Steps into the Blessed Life

Sermons on Christian Living - Moral, Practical and Biblical

By F. B. Meyer

PANTIANOS
CLASSICS

Published by Pantianos Classics

ISBN-13: 978-1-78987-484-6

First published in 1896

Contents

The First Step into the Blessed Life

THERE is a Christian life, which, in comparison with that experienced by the majority of Christians, is as summer to winter, or, as the mature fruitfulness of a golden autumn to the struggling promise of a cold and late spring. It is such a life as Caleb might have lived in Hebron, the city of Fellowship; or the Apostle John was living, when he wrote his epistles. It may be fitly termed the Blessed Life.

And the Blessedness of the Blessed Life lies in this: that we trust the Lord to do in us and for us what we could not do; and we find that He does not belie His word, but that, according to our faith, so it is done to us. The weary spirit, which has vainly sought to realize its ideal by its own strivings and efforts, now gives itself over to the strong and tender hands of the Lord Jesus; and He accepts the task; and at once begins to work in it to will and to do of His own good pleasure, delivering it from the tyranny of besetting sin, and fulfilling in it His own perfect ideal.

This Blessed Life should be the normal life of every Christian; in work and rest; in the building-up of the inner life, and in the working-out of the life-plan. It is God's thought not for a few, but for all His children. The youngest and weakest may lay claim to it, equally with the strongest and oldest. We should step into it at the moment of conversion; without wandering with blistered feet, for forty years in the desert; or lying, for thirty-eight years, with disappointed hopes, in the porch of the House of Mercy.

But since many have long ago passed the moment of conversion, without entering the Blessed Life, it may be well to show clearly, what the first step must be, to take us within its golden circle. Better take it late than never.

The first step into the Blessed Life is contained in the one word,

"Consecration;"

And is enforced by the significant exhortation of the Apostle (Rom. vi. 13).

It is not enough to give our time, or energy, or money. Many will gladly give anything, rather than *themselves.* But none of these will be accounted as a sufficient substitute by Him, who gave, not only His possessions, but His very Self for us. As the Lord Jesus was all for us. He asks that we should be all for Him. Body, soul, and spirit; one reasonable service and gift.

That Consecration is the stepping-stone to Blessedness, is clearly established in the experience of God's children. For instance, Frances Ridley Havergal has left us this record: "It was on Advent Sunday, December, 1873, that I first saw clearly the blessedness of true consecration. I saw it as a flash of electric light, and what you see you can never unsee. *There must be full surrender before there can be full Blessedness. God admits you by the one into the other.*

First I was shown that the body of Jesus Christ, His Son, cleanseth from all sin; and then it was made plain to me that He who had thus cleansed me, had power to keep me clean; *so I utterly yielded myself to Him and utterly trusted Him to keep me.*"

The seraphic Whitfield, the brothers Wesley, the great Welsh preacher Christmas Evans, the French pastor Oberlin, and many more have given the same testimony. And in their mouths surely this truth may be regarded as established, that we must pass through Gilgal to the Land of Rest; and that the strait gate of Consecration alone leads into the Blessed Life.

1. — *The ground of Consecration is in the great Scripture statement that we are Christ's.* There is a two-fold ground of proprietorship. *We are His by Purchase*, "Ye are not your own, for ye are bought with a price." Step into that slave-market, where men and women are waiting like chattels to be bought. Yonder comes a wealthy planter, who, after due examination, lays down his money for a number of men and women to stock his estate. From that moment, those persons are absolutely his property, as much so as his cattle or his sheep. All they possess, all they may earn, is absolutely his. So, the Apostles reasoned, they were Christ's; and often they began their epistles by calling themselves, "the slaves of Jesus Christ." Paul went so far as to say that he bore in his body the brand-marks of Jesus. And are not all Christians Christ's, whether they own it and live up to it, or not; because He purchased them by His most precious blood? *We are His also by Deed of Gift.* The Father has given to the Son all who shall come to Him. If ever you have come, or shall come, to Jesus Christ as your Saviour, you show that you have been included in that wonderful donation (John vi. 37). And is it likely that the Father gave only a part of us? Nay, as utterly as He gave His Son for us, so hath He given us to His Son. And our Lord Jesus thinks much of that solemn transaction, though we, alas! often live as if it had never taken place, and were free to live as we pleased.

2. — *The Act of Consecration is to recognize Christ's ownership; and to accept it; and to say to Him with the whole heart, Lord, I am Thine by Eighty and I wish to be Thine by Choice.* Of old the mighty men of Israel were willing to swim the rivers at their flood, to come to David, their un-crowned but God-appointed King. And when they met him, they cried, "Thine are we, David, and on thy side, thou son of Jesse." They were his because God had given them to him, but they could not rest content till they were his also by their glad choice. Why then should we not say the same to Jesus Christ? "Lord Jesus, I am Thine by right; forgive me that I have lived so long as if I were my own; and now I gladly recognize that Thou hast a rightful claim on all I have and am; I want to live as Thine from henceforth; and I do solemnly and at this hour give myself to Thee. Thine in life and death. Thine absolutely and forever."

Do not try to make a covenant with God, lest you should break it, and be discouraged. But quietly fall into your right attitude as one who belongs to

Christ. Take as your motto the noble confession, "Whose I am and whom I serve." Breathe the grand old simple lines: —

> "Just as I am, — Thy love unknown
> Has broken every barrier down;
> *Now to be Thine, yea, Thine alone,*
>   *O Lamb of God, I come.*"

3. — *Consecration is not the act of our feelings, but of our will.* Do not try to feel anything. Do not try to make yourself fit or good or earnest enough for Christ. God is working in you to will, whether you feel it or not. He is giving you power, at this moment, to will and do His good pleasure. Believe this, and act upon it at once; and say, "Lord Jesus, I am willing to be Thine;" or, if you cannot say as much as that, say, "Lord Jesus, I am willing to be made willing to be Thine for evermore."

Consecration is only possible, when we give up our will *about everything.* As soon as we come to the point of giving ourselves to God, we are almost certain to become aware of the presence of one thing, if not of more, out of harmony with His will. And whilst we feel able to surrender ourselves in all other points, here we exercise reserve. Every room and cupboard in the house, with the exception of this, thrown open to the new occupant. Every limb in the body but one, submitted to the practiced hand of the Good Physician. But that small reserve spoils the whole. To give ninety-nine parts and to withhold the hundredth undoes the whole transaction. Jesus will have all or none. And He is wise. Who would live in a fever-stricken house, so long as one room was not exposed to disinfectants, air, and sun? Who would undertake a case so long as the patient refused to submit one part of his body to examination? Who would become responsible for a bankrupt so long as one ledger was kept back? The reason that so many fail to attain the Blessed Life is that there is some one point in which they hold back from God; and concerning which they prefer to have their own way and will rather than His. In this one thing they will not yield their will and accept God's; and this one little thing mars the whole, robs them of peace, and compels them to wander in the desert.

4. — *If you cannot give all, ask the Lord Jesus to TAKE all, and especially that which seems so hard to give.* Many have been helped by hearing it put thus. Tell them to give, and they shake their heads despondently. They are like the little child who told her mother that she had been trying to give Jesus her heart, *but it wouldn't go.* But ask them if they are willing for Him to come into their hearts, and take all; and they will joyfully assent.

Tennyson says: — "Our wills are ours to make them Thine." But sometimes it seems impossible to shape them out so as to match every corner and angle of the Will of God. What a relief it is at such a moment to hand the will over to Christ; telling Him *that we are willing to be made willing* to have His will in all things; and asking Him to melt our stubborn waywardness, to fashion our wills upon His anvil, and to bring us into perfect accord with Himself.

5. — *When we are willing that the Lord Jesus should take all, we must believe that He does take all.* He does not wait for us to free ourselves from evil habits; or to make ourselves good; or to feel glad and happy. His one desire is that we should put our will, on His side, in everything. When this is done He *instantly* enters the surrendered heart, and begins His blessed work of renovation and renewal. From the very moment of consecration, though it be done in much feebleness, and with slender appreciation of its entire meaning, the spirit may begin to say with new emphasis, "I am His, I am His, Glory to God, I am His." Directly the gift is laid on the altar, the fire falls on it.

Sometimes there is a rush of holy feeling. It was so with James Brained Taylor, who tells, "I felt that I needed something I did not possess. I desired it, not for my benefit only, but for that of the Church and the world. I lifted up my heart that the blessing might descend. At this juncture I was delightfully conscious of giving up all to God. I was enabled in my heart to say, "*Here Lord, take me, take my whole soul, and seal me Thine now, and Thine for ever. If Thou wilt Thou canst make me clean.* Then there ensued such emotions as I never before experienced. All was calm and tranquil, and a heaven of love pervaded my soul. I had the witness of God's love to me, and of mine to Him. Shortly after I was dissolved in tears of love and gratitude to our blessed Lord,, who came as King, and took possession of my heart."

It is very delightful when such emotions are given to us; but we must not look for them, or depend on them. Our consecration may be accepted, and may excite the liveliest joy in our Saviour's heart, though we are filled with no answering ecstasy. We may know that the great transaction is done, without any glad outburst of song. We may even have to exercise faith, against feeling, as we say, many scores of times each day, "I am His." But the absence of feeling proves nothing. And we must pillow our heads on the conviction that Jesus took what we gave, at the moment of our giving it; and that He will keep that which was committed to Him, against that day.

6. — *It is well to make the act of consecration a definite one in our spiritual history.* George Whitfield did it in the ordination service. "I can call heaven and earth to witness that, when the Bishop laid his hand upon me, I gave myself up to be a martyr for Him who hung upon the cross for me. Known unto Him are all the future events and contingencies. I have thrown myself blindfolded, and without reserve, into His Almighty hands."

Christmas Evans did it as he was climbing a lonely and mountainous road toward Cader Idris. "I was weary of a cold heart toward Christ, and began to pray, and soon felt the fetters loosening, tears flowed copiously, and I was constrained to cry out for the gracious visits of God. Thus I resigned myself to Christ, body and soul, gifts and labors, all my life, every day and every hour that remained to me; and all my cares I committed to Christ."

Stephen Grellet did it in the woods. "The woods are there of lofty and large pines, and my mind being inwardly retired before the Lord, He was pleased so to reveal His love to me through His blessed Son, my Saviour, that my fears were removed, my wounds healed, my mourning turned into joy; and He strengthened me to offer up myself freely to him and to His service, for my whole life."

It matters little when and how we do it; whether by speech or in writing; whether alone or in company; but we must not be content with a general desire; we must come to a definite act, at a given moment of time, when we shall gladly acknowledge and confess Christ's absolute ownership of all we are and have.

7. — *When the act of consecration is once truly done, it need not be repeated.* We may review it with thankfulness. We may add some new codicils to it. We may learn how much more was involved in it than we ever dreamed. We may find new departments of our being, constantly demanding to be included. But we cannot undo, and need never repeat it; and if we fall away from it, let us go at once to our merciful High-Priest, confessing our sin, and seeking forgiveness and restoration.

8. — *The advantages resulting from this act cannot be enumerated here.* They pass all count. The first and best is the special filling by the Holy Grhost; and as He fills the heart, He drives before him the evil things which had held possession there too long; just as mercury, poured into a glass of water, sinks to the bottom, expels the water, and takes its place. Directly we give ourselves to Christ, He seals us by His Spirit. Directly we present Him with a yielded nature. He begins to fill it with the Holy Ghost. Let us not try to feel that it is so. Let us believe that it is so; and reckon on God's faithfulness. Others will soon see a marked difference in us, though we wist it not.

9. — *All that we have to do is to maintain this attitude of full surrender, by the grace of the Holy Spirit.* Remember that Jesus Christ offered Himself to God, through the *Eternal Spirit;* and He waits to do as much for you. Ask Him to maintain you in this attitude, and to maintain this attitude in you. Use regularly the means of meditation, private prayer, and Bible study. Seek forgiveness for any failure, directly you are conscious of it; and ask to be restored. Practice the holy habit of the constant recollection of God. Do not be eager to work for God, but let God work through you. Accept everything that happens to you as being permitted, and therefore sent by the will of Him who loves you infinitely. And there will roll in upon you wave on wave, tide on tide, ocean on ocean of an experience, fitly called the Blessed Life, because it is full of the Happiness of the ever-blessed God Himself.

Dear reader, will you not take this step? There will be no further difficulty about money, dress, or amusements, or similar questions, which perplex some. Your heart will be filled and satisfied with the true riches. As the willing slave of Jesus Christ, you will only seek to do the will of your great and gentle Master. To spend every coin as He directs. To act as His steward. To dress so as to give Him pleasure. To spend the time only as He may approve. To do His will on earth, as it is in heaven. All this will come easy and delightful.

You are perhaps far from this at present. But it is all within your reach. Do not be afraid of Christ. He wants to take nothing from you, except that which you would give up at once, if you could see, as clearly as He does, the harm it is inflicting. He will ask of you nothing inconsistent with the most perfect fitness and tenderness. He will give you grace enough to perform every duty He may demand. "His yoke is easy; His burden is light."

Blessed Spirit of God, by whom alone human words can be made to speak to the heart, deign to use these, to point to many a longing soul the First Step into the Blessed Life, for the exceeding Glory of the Lord Jesus, and for the sake of a dying world.

The Secret of Guidance

MANY children of God are so deeply-exercised on the matter of guidance that it may be helpful to give a few suggestions as to knowing the way in which our Father would have us walk, and the work he would have us do. The importance of the subject cannot be exaggerated; so much of our power and peace consists in knowing where God would have us be, and in being just there.

The manna only falls where the cloudy pillar broods; but it is certain to be found on the sands, which a few hours ago were glistening in the flashing light of the heavenly fire, and are now shadowed by the fleecy canopy of cloud. If we are precisely where our heavenly Father would have us to be, we are perfectly sure that He will provide food and raiment, and everything beside. When He sends His servants to Cherith, He will make even the ravens to bring them food.

How much of our Christian work has been abortive, because we have persisted in initiating it for ourselves, instead of ascertaining what God was doing, and where He required our presence. We dream bright dreams of success. We try and command it. We call to our aid all kinds of expedients, questionable or otherwise. And at last we turn back, disheartened and ashamed, like children who are torn and scratched by the brambles, and soiled by the quagmire. None of this had come about, if only we had been, from the first, under God's unerring guidance. He might test us, but he could not allow us to mistake.

Naturally, the child of God, longing to know his Father's will, turns to the sacred Book, and refreshes his confidence by noticing how in all ages God has guided those who dared to trust Him up to the very hilt, but who, at the time, must have been as perplexed as we are often now. We know how Abraham left kindred and country, and started, with no other guide than God, across the trackless desert to a land which he knew not. We know how for forty years the Israelites were led through the peninsula of Sinai, with its labyrinths of red sand-stone and its wastes of sand. We know how Joshua, in entering the Land of Promise, was able to cope with the difficulties of an unknown region, and to overcome great and warlike nations, because he looked to the Captain of the Lord's host, who ever leads to victory. We know how, in the earl}' Church, the Apostles were enabled to thread their way through the most difficult questions, and to solve the most perplexing problems; laying down principles which will guide the Church to the end of time; and this because it was revealed to them as to what they should do and say, by the Holy Spirit.

The promises for guidance are unmistakable, Psalm xxxii. 8: "I will instruct thee and teach thee in the way which thou shalt go." This is God's distinct assurance to those whose transgressions are forgiven, and whose sins are covered, and who are more quick to notice the least symptom of His will, than horse or mule to feel the bit.

Prov. iii. 6: "In all thy ways acknowledge Him, and He shall direct (or make plain) thy paths." A sure word, on which we may rest; if only we fulfil the previous conditions, of trusting with all our heart, and of not leaning to our own understanding."

Isa. lviii. 11: "The Lord shall guide thee continually." It is impossible to think that He could guide us at all, if He did not guide us always. For the greatest events of life, like the huge rocking-stones in the west of England, revolve on the smallest points. A pebble may alter the flow of a stream. The growth of a grain of mustard seed may determine the rainfall of a continent. Thus we are bidden to look for a Guidance which shall embrace the whole of life in all its myriad necessities.

John viii. 12: "I am the light of the world; he that followeth Me shall not walk in darkness, but shall have the light of life." The reference here seems to be to the wilderness wanderings; and the Master promises to be to all faithful souls, in their pilgrimage to the City of God, what the cloudy pillar was to the children of Israel on their march to the Land of Promise.

These are but specimens. The vault of Scripture is inlaid with thousands such, that glisten in their measure as the stars which guide the wanderer across the deep. Well may the prophet sum up the heritage of the servants of the Lord by saying of the Holy City, "All thy children shall be taught of the Lord, and great shall be the peace of thy children."

And yet it may appear to some tried and timid hearts as if every one mentioned in the Word of God was helped, but they are left without help. They seem to have Stood before perplexing problems, face to face with life's mysteries, eagerly longing to know what to do, but no angel has come to tell them, and no iron gate has opened to them in the prison-house of circumstances.

Some lay the blame on their own stupidity. Their minds are blunt and dull. They cannot catch God's meaning, which would be clear to others. They are so nervous of doing wrong, that they cannot learn clearly what is right. "Who is blind, but my servant? or deaf, as my messenger that I sent? Who is blind as he that is perfect, and blind as the Lord's servant?" Yet, how do we treat our children? One child is so bright-witted and so keen that a little hint is enough to indicate the way; another was born dull: it cannot take in your meaning quickly. Do you only let the clever one know what you want? AA ill you not take the other upon your knee and make clear to it the directions which baffle it? Does not the distress of the tiny nursling, who longs to know that it may immediately obey, weave an almost stronger bond than that which binds you to the rest? Oh! weary, perplexed, and stupid children, believe in the great love of God, and cast yourselves upon it, sure that he will come down to your ignorance, and suit Himself to your needs, and will take "the lambs in His arms, and carry them in His bosom, and *gently lead* those that are with young."

There are certain practical directions which we must attend to in order that we may be led into the mind of the Lord.

1. — *Our Motives must he Pure,* "When thine eye is single, thy whole body is also full of light" (Luke xi. 34). You have been much in darkness lately, and perhaps this passage will point the reason. Your eye has not been single. There has been some obliquity of vision. A spiritual squint. And this has hindered you from discerning indications of God's will, which otherwise had been as clear as noonday.

We must be very careful in judging our motives: searching them as the detectives at the doors of the House of Commons search each stranger who enters. When, by the grace of God, we have been delivered from grosser forms of sin, we are still liable to the subtle working of self in our holiest and loveliest hours. It poisons our motives. It breathes decay on our fairest fruit-bearing. It whispers seductive flatteries into our pleased ears. It turns the spirit from its holy purpose as the masses of iron on ocean steamers deflect the needle of the compass from the pole.

So long as there is some thought of personal advantage, some idea of acquiring the praise and commendation of men, some aim at self-aggrandizement, it will be simply impossible to find out God's purpose concerning us. The door must be resolutely shut against all this, if we would hear the still small voice. All cross-lights must be excluded, if we would see the Urim and Thummim stone brighten with God's "Yes," or darken with his "No."

Ask the Holy Spirit to give you the single eye, and to inspire in your heart one aim alone; that which animated our Lord, and enabled Him to cry, as He reviewed His life, "I have glorified Thee on earth." Let this be the watchword of our lives, "Glory to God in the highest." Then our "whole body shall be full of light, having no part dark, as when the bright shining of a candle doth give light."

2. — *Our Will must be Surrendered.* "My judgment is just; because I seek not Mine own will, but the will of the Father which hath sent Me" (John v. 30). This was the secret, which Jesus not only practiced, but taught. In one form or another He was constantly insisting on a surrendered will, as the key to perfect knowledge, "If any man will do His will, he shall know."

There is all the difference between a will which is extinguished and one which is surrendered. God does not demand that our wills should be crushed out, like the sinews of a fakir's unused arm. He only asks that they should say "Yes" to Him. Pliant to Him as the willow twig to the practiced hand.

Many a time, as the steamer has neared the quay, have I watched the little lad take his place beneath the poop, with eye and ear fixed on the captain, and waiting to shout each word he utters to the grimy engineers below; and often have I longed that my will should repeat as accurately, and as promptly, the words and will of God, that all the lower nature might obey.

It is for the lack of this subordination that we so often miss the guidance we seek. There is a secret controversy between our will and God's. And we shall never be right till we have let Him take, and break, and make. Oh! do seek for that. If you cannot give, let Him take. If you are not willing, confess that you are willing to be made willing. Hand yourself over to Him to work in you, to will and to do of His own good pleasure. We must be as plastic clay, ready to take any shape that the great Potter may choose, so shall we be able to detect His guidance.

3. — *We must seek Information for our Mind.* This is certainly the next step. God has given us these wonderful faculties of brain power, and He will not ignore them. In the days of the Reformation He did not destroy the Roman Catholic churches or pulpits; He did better. He preached in them. And in grace He does not cancel the action of any of His marvelous bestowments, but He uses them for the communication of His purposes and thoughts.

It is of the greatest importance, then, that we should feed our minds with facts; with reliable information; with the results of human experience, and above all, with the teachings of the Word of God. It is matter for the utmost admiration to notice how full the Bible is of biography and history: so that there is hardly a single crisis in our lives that may not be matched from those wondrous pages. There is no book like the Bible for casting a light on the dark landings of human life.

We have no need or right to run hither and thither to ask our friends what we ought to do; but there is no harm in our taking pains to gather all reliable information, on which the flame of holy thought and consecrated purpose may feed and grow strong. It is for us ultimately to decide as God shall teach us, but His voice may come to us through the voice of sanctified common-sense, acting on the materials we have collected. Of course at times God may bid us act against our reason; but these are very exceptional; and then our duty will be so clear that there can be no mistake. But for the most part God will speak in the results of deliberate consideration, weighing and balancing the *pros* and *cons*.

When Peter was shut up in prison, and could not possibly extricate himself, an angel was sent to do for him what he could not do for himself; but when they had passed through a street or two of the city, the angel left him to consider the matter for himself. Thus God treats us still. He will dictate a miraculous course by miraculous methods. But when the ordinary light of reason is adequate to the task, He will leave us to act as occasion may serve.

4. — *We must be much in Prayer for Guidance*. The Psalms are full of earnest pleadings for clear direction: "Show me Thy way, O Lord, lead me in a plain path, because of mine enemies." It is the law of our Father's house that His children shall ask for what they want. "If any man lack wisdom, let him ask of God, who giveth to all men liberally, and upbraideth not."

In a time of change and crisis, we need to be much in prayer, not only on our knees, but in that sweet form of inward prayer, in which the spirit is constantly offering itself up to God, asking to be shown His will; soliciting that it may be impressed upon its surface, as the heavenly bodies photograph themselves on prepared paper. Wrapt in prayer like this the truthful believer may tread the deck of the ocean steamer night after night, sure that He who points the stars their courses will not fail to direct the soul which has no other aim than to do His will.

One good form of prayer at such a juncture is to ask that doors may be shut, that the way may be closed, and that all enterprises which are not according to God's will may be arrested at their very beginning. Put the matter absolutely into God's hands from the outset, and He will not fail to shatter the project and defeat the aim which is not according to His holy will.

5. — *We must wait the gradual Unfolding of God's Plan in Providence*. God's impressions within and His word without are always corroborated by His Providence around, and we should quietly wait until these three focus into one point.

Sometimes it looks as if we are bound to act. Every one says we must do something; and indeed things seem to have reached so desperate a pitch that we must. Behind are the Egyptians; right and left are inaccessible precipices; before is the sea. It is not easy at such times to stand still and see the salvation of God; but we must. When Saul compelled himself, and offered sacrifice, because he thought that Samuel was too late in coming, he made the great mistake of his life.

God may delay to come in the guise of His Providence. There was delay ere Sennacherib's host lay like withered leaves around the Holy City. There was delay ere Jesus came walking on the sea in the early dawn, or hastened to raise Lazarus. There was delay ere the angel sped to Peter's side on the night before his expected martyrdom. He stays long enough to test patience of faith, but not a moment behind the extreme hour of need. "The vision is yet for an appointed time, but at the end it shall speak, and shall not lie; though it tarry, wait for it; because it will surely come; it will not tarry."

It is very remarkable how God guides us by circumstances. At one moment the way may seem utterly blocked, and then shortly afterwards some trivial incident occurs, which might not seem much to others, but which to the keen eye of faith speaks volumes. Sometimes these signs are repeated in different ways in answer to prayer. They are not haphazard results of chance, but the opening up of circumstances in the direction in which we should walk. And they begin to multiply, as we advance towards our goal, just as lights do as we near a populous town, when darting through the land by night express.

Sometimes men sigh for an angel to come to point them their way: that simply indicates that as yet the time has not come for them to move. If you do not know what you ought to do, stand still until you do. And when the time comes for action, circumstances, like glow-worms, will sparkle along your path; and you will become so sure that you are right, when God's three witnesses concur, that you could not be surer though an angel beckoned you on.

The circumstances of our daily life are to us an infallible indication of God's will, when they concur with the inward promptings of the Spirit and with the Word of God. So long as they are stationary, wait. When you must act, they will open, and a way will be made through oceans and rivers, wastes and rocks.

We often make a great mistake, thinking that God is not guiding us at all, because we cannot see far in front. But this is not His method. He only undertakes that *the steps* of a good man should be ordered by the Lord. Not next year, but to-morrow. Not the next mile, but the next yard. Not the whole pattern, but the next stitch in the canvas. If you expect more than this you will be disappointed, and get back into the dark. But this will secure for you leading in the right way, as you will acknowledge when you review it from the hilltops of glory.

We cannot ponder too deeply the lessons of the cloud given in the exquisite picture-lesson on Guidance (Num. ix. 15-23). Let us look high enough for guidance. Let us encourage our soul to wait only upon God till it is given. Let us cultivate that meekness which He will guide in judgment. Let us seek to be of quick understanding, that we may be apt to see the least sign of His will. Let us stand with girded loins and lighted lamps, that we may be prompt to obey. Blessed are those servants. They shall be led by a right way to the golden city of the saints.

Speaking for myself, after months of waiting and prayer, I have become absolutely sure of the Guidance of my heavenly Father; and with the emphasis of personal experience, I would encourage each troubled and perplexed soul that may read these lines to wait patiently for the Lord, until He clearly indicates His will.

The Chambers of the King

CHRISTIAN experience may be compared to a suite of royal apartments, of which the first opens into the second, and that again into the third, and so on. It is, of course, true that believers enter on a possession of all so soon as they are born into the royal, divine household. But, as a matter of fact, certain truths stand out more clearly to them at different stages of their history, and thus their successive experiences may be compared to the chambers of a palace, through which they pass to the throne-room and presence-chamber of their King. And the King Himself is waiting at the threshold to act as guide. The key is in His hand, which opens, and no man shuts; which shuts, and no man opens. Have you entered the first of those chambers? If not. He waits to unlock the first door of all to you at this moment, and to lead you forward from stage to stage, till you have realized all that can be enjoyed by saintly hearts on this side the gates of pearl.

Only be sure to follow where Jesus leads the way. "Draw me, we will run after Thee" (Sol. Song i. 4).

THE FIRST CHAMBER IN THE KING'S HOLY PALACE IS THE CHAMBER OF THE NEW BIRTH

In some cases it is preceded by a portico, known as Conviction for Sin. But as the portico is not part of the house, and all do not pass through it, we need not stay further to describe it. Over the door of this chamber are inscribed the words: "Except a man be born again, he cannot enter" (John iii. 3-5).

By nature we are destitute of life — *dead in trespasses and sins*. We need, therefore, first, not a new creed, but a new life. The prophet's staff is well enough where there is life; but it is useless on the face of a dead babe. The first requisite is *Life*. This is what the Holy Spirit gives us at the moment of conversion. He comes to us through some truth of the incorruptible Word of God, and implants the first spark of the new life; and we who were dead, live. Thus we enter the first room in our Father's palace, where the new-born babes are welcomed and nursed and fed.

We may remember the day and place of our new birth, or we may be as ignorant of them as of the circumstances of our natural birth. But what does it matter that a man cannot recall his birthday, so long as he knows that he is alive?

As an outstretched hand has two sides — the upper, called *the back;* the under, called *the palm* — so there are two sides and names for the act of entrance into the Chamber of the New Birth. Angels, looking at it from the heaven side, call it *being born again*. Men, looking at it from the earth side, call it *trusting Jesus*. "Those that believe in His name are born;" "Those that receive Him have the right to become the sons of God" (John i. 12, 13). If you are born again, you will trust. And if you are trusting Jesus, however many your doubts and fears, you are certainly born again, and have entered the palace. If you go no further, you will be saved, but you will miss untold blessedness.

From the chamber of birth, where the new-born ones rejoice together, realizing for the first time the throbbing of the life of God, there is a door leading into a second chamber, which may be called

THE CHAMBER OF ASSURANCE

And over that door of entrance, where the King awaits us with beckoning hand, these words are engraved: "Beloved, now are we the sons of God" (1 John iii. 2). In many cases, of course, assurance follows immediately on conversion, as a father's kiss on his words of forgiveness to the penitent child. But it is also true, that there are some souls, truly saved, who pass through weeks, months, and sometimes years, without being sure of their standing in Jesus, or deriving any comfort from it.

True assurance comes from the work of the Holy Spirit through the sacred Scriptures. Read the Word looking for His teaching. Think ten times of Christ for every once of yourself. Dwell much on all references to His finished work. Understand that you are so truly one with Him, that you died in Him, lay with Him in the garden tomb, rose with Him, ascended with Him back to God, and have been already welcomed and accepted in the Beloved (Eph. ii. 5, 6). Remember that His Father is your Father, and that you are a son in the Son; and as you dwell on these truths, opening your heart to the Holy Spirit, He will pervade your soul with a blessed conviction that you have eternal life, and that you are a child, not because you feel it, but because God says so (John iii. 36; Rom. viii. 16).

The door at the further end of this apartment leads into another chamber of the King. It is the door of consecration, leading into the

CHAMBER OF A SURRENDERED WILL

Above the doorway stand the words: "From henceforth let no man trouble me: for I bear branded on my body the marks of Jesus; whose I am, and whom I serve" (Gal. vi. 17, R. V.; and Acts xxvii. 23). Consecration is giving Jesus His own. We are His by right, because He bought us with His blood. *But, alas, He has not had His money's worth!* He paid for all, and He has had but a fragment of our energy, time, and earnings. By an act of consecration, let us ask Him to forgive the robbery of the past, and let us profess our desire to be henceforth utterly and only for Him; His slaves, His chattels, owning no master than Himself.

As soon as we say this, He will test our sincerity, as He did the young ruler's, by asking something of us. He will lay His finger on something within us which He wants us to alter, obeying some command, or abstaining from some indulgence. If we instantly give up our will and way to Him, we pass the narrow doorway into the Chamber of Surrender, which has a southern aspect, and is ever warm and radiant with His presence, because obedience is the condition of manifested love (John xiv. 23).

This doorway is very narrow, and entrance is only possible for fchose who will lay aside weights as well as sins. A weight is anything which, without being essentially wrong or hurtful to others, is yet a hindrance to ourselves. We may always know a weight by three signs: *first,* we are uneasy about it; *second,* we argue for it against our conscience; *third,* we go about asking people's advice, whether we may not keep it without harm. All these things must be laid aside in the strength which Jesus waits to give. Ask Him to deal with them for you, that you may be set in joint *in every good work* to do His will (Heb. xiii. 21).

At the further end of this apartment another door invites us to enter

THE CHAMBER OF THE FILLING OF THE SPIRIT

And above the entrance glisten the words, "Be filled with the Spirit" (Eph. v. 18). We gladly admit that the Holy Spirit is literally in the heart of every true believer (Rom. viii. 9); and that the whole work of grace in our souls is due to Him, from the first desire to be saved to the last prayer breathed on the threshold of heaven. But it is also true that a period comes in our education, when we become more alive to the necessity of the Holy Spirit, and seek for more of his all-pervading heart-filling presence.

Many of us have lately been startled to find that we have been content with too little of the Holy Spirit. There has been enough throne-water to cover the stones in the river-bed, but not to fill its channel. Instead of occupying all, our gracious Guest has been confined to one or two back rooms of our hearts; as a poor housekeeper is sometimes put in to keep a mansion, dwelling in attic or cellar; while the suites of splendid apartments are consigned to dust-sheets and cobwebs, shuttered, dismantled, and locked.

Each Christian has the Holy Spirit; but each Christian needs more and more of Him, until the whole nature is filled, nay, it would be truer to say, the Holy Spirit wants more and more of us. Let us ask our heavenly Father to give us of His Spirit in ever enlarging measures; and as we ask, let us yield ourselves incessantly to His indwelling and in working. Then let us believe that we are filled, not because we feel it, but because we are sure that God is keeping His word with us: "Ye shall not see wind, neither shall ye see rain; yet that valley shall be filled with water."

It is true that the filling of the Spirit involves separation, a giving up, a going apart, which is keenly bitter to the flesh. The filling of Pentecost is a baptism of fire. But there is joy amid the flames as the bonds shrivel, and the limbs are free, and the Son of God walks beside.

But this chamber leads to another of exceeding blessedness.

THE CHAMBER OF ABIDING IN CHRIST

Around the doorway a vine is sculptured with trailing branches and pendent grapes; and, entwined among the foliage, these words appear: "Abide in Me, and I in you" (John xv. 4). The Holy Spirit never reveals Himself. Those who have most of His grace, "wist it not." His chosen work is to reveal the Lord. We are not conscious of the Spirit, but of Him who is the Alpha and Omega of our life. Christ's loveliness fills the soul, where the Spirit is in full possession, as the odor of the ointment filled the house at Bethany.

Our Lord is with us all the days; but often our eyes are holden, that we do not know Him; and if for a radiant moment we discern Him, He vanishes from our sight. There is an experience which we do not only *believe* that He is near, but we *perceive* His presence by the instinct of the heart. He becomes a living, bright reality; sitting by our hearth, walking beside us through the crowded streets, sailing with us across the stormy lake, standing beside the graves that hold our dead, sharing our crosses and our burdens, turning the water of common joys into the wine of holy sacraments.

Then the believer leans hard on the ever-present Lord, drawing on His fulness, appropriating His unsearchable riches, claiming from Him grace to turn every temptation into the means of increasing likeness to Himself. And if the branch abide constantly in the Vine, it cannot help bearing fruit; nay, the difficulty would be to keep fruit back.

We have to do with the death and not with the life part of our experience (Rom. viii. 13). The oftener we sow ourselves in the clods of daily self-denial, falling into the furrows to die, the more fruit we bear. It is by always bearing about in the body the dying of the Lord Jesus, that the life of Jesus is made manifest in our mortal flesh. Prune off every bud on the old stock, and all the energy will pass up to the rare flowers and fruits grafted there by Heaven.

But see the King beckons us forward to pass onwards into

THE CHAMBER OF VICTORY OYER SIN

Above the door are the words: "Whosoever abideth in Him sinneth not" (1 John iii. 6). Around the walls hang various instruments of war (Eph. vi. 13); and frescoes of the over-comers receiving the fair rewards which the King hath promised (Rev. ii., iii). We must be careful of the order in which we put these things. Many seek victory over sin before yielding themselves entirely to God. But you can never enter this chamber, where the palm-branch waves, unless you have passed through the chamber of consecration.

Give yourself wholly up to Jesus, and He will keep you. Will you dare to say, that He can hold the oceans in the hollow of His hand, and sustain the arch of heaven, and fill the sun with light for millenniums, but that He cannot keep

18

you from being overcome by sin, or filled with the impetuous rush of unholy passion? Can He not deliver His saints from the sword. His darlings from the power of the dog? Is all power given Him in heaven and on earth, and must He stand paralyzed before the devils that possess you, unable to cast them out? To ask such questions is to answer them. "I am persuaded He is able to keep" (2 Tim. i. 12; 1 John v. 11).

We may expect to be tempted till we die. We certainly shall carry about with us an evil nature, which would manifest itself, unless kept in check by the grace of God. But if we abide in Christ, and He abide in us, if we live under the power of the Holy Spirit, temptation will excite no fascination in us, but, on the contrary, horror; the least stirring of our self-life will be instantly noticed, and met by the Name and Blood and Spirit of Jesus; the tides of His purity and life will flow so strongly over our being as to sweep away any black drops of ink oozing upwards from the sand.

You must, however, irrevocably shut the back door, as well as the front door, against sin. You must not dally with it as possible in any form. You must see that you are shut up to saintliness by the purpose of God (Rom. viii. 29). You must definitely and forever elect the cross as the destiny of your self-life. And you will find that He will save you from all that you dare to trust Him with. "Everyplace that the sole of your foot shall tread upon, that have I given unto thee." And His work within is most perfect when it is least apparent; and when the flesh is kept so utterly in abeyance that we begin to think it has been altogether extracted.

Yet another door, at the far end of this chamber, summons us to advance to

THE CHAMBER OF HEART REST

The King Himself spoke its motto-text: "Take My yoke, and ye shall find rest unto your souls" (Matt. xi. 29). Soft strains float on the air; the peace of God stands sentry against intruding care. Of course the soul learnt something of rest at the very outset. But those words of the Master indicate that there are at least two kinds of rest. And so the rest of forgiveness passes into the rest of surrender and satisfaction.

We lay our worries and cares where once we only laid our sins. We lose the tumultuous fever and haste of earlier days. We become oblivious to praise on the one hand and censure on the other. Our soul is poised on God, satisfied with God, seeks nothing outside God, regards all things from the standpoint of eternity and of God. The life loses the babble of its earlier course, and sweeps onwards to the ocean, from which it derived its being, with a stillness which bespeaks its depth, a serenity which foretells its destiny. The very face tells the tale of the sweet, still life within, which is attuned to the everlasting chime of the land where storms come not, nor conflict, nor alarm.

Some say that the door at the end of this chamber leads into the chamber of

It may be so. All along the Christian's course there is a great and growing love for the world for which He died. But there are times when that love amounts almost to an agony of compassion and desire; and there come sufferings caused by the thorn-crown, the sneer, the mockery, the cross, the spear, the baptism of blood and tears. All these fall to the lot of the followers of the King; and perhaps they come most plentifully to the saintliest, the likest to the Lord.

But certain it is that those who suffer thus are they who reign. Their sufferings are not for a moment to be compared to the glory revealed in their lives. And out of their bitter griefs, sweetened by the Cross, gush water-springs to refresh the weary heritage of God, like the waters of the Exodus (Exod. xv. 25).

Beyond all these, and separated from them by a very slight interval, are the

MANSIONS OF THE FATHER'S HOUSE

into which the King will lead us presently, chamber after chamber of delight, stretch after stretch of golden glory, until these natures, which are but as an infant's, have developed to the measure of the stature of our full growth, unto the likeness of the Son of God.

O soul! where have you got to? Do not linger inside the first chamber, but press on and forward. If any door seems locked, knock, and it shall be opened unto you. Never consider that you have attained, or are already perfect, but follow on to apprehend all that for which Jesus Christ apprehended you.

In the Secret of His Presence

In one sense God is always near us. He is not an Absentee, needing to be brought down from the heavens or up from the deep. He is nigh at hand. His Being pervades all being. Every world, that floats like an islet in the ocean of space, is filled with signs of His presence, just as the home of your friend is littered with the many evidences of his residence, by which you know that he lives there, though you have not seen his face. Every crocus pushing through the dark mould; every fire-fly in the forest; every bird that springs up from its nest before your feet; everything that is — all are as full of God's presence, as the bush which burned with His fire, before which Moses bared his feet in acknowledgment that God was there.

But we do not always realize it. We often pass hours, and days, and weeks; we sometimes engage in seasons of prayer; we go to and fro from His house, where the ladder of communion rests; and still He is a shadow, a name, a tradition, a dream of days gone by.

"Oh! that I knew where I might find Him, that I might come even to His seat. Behold! I go forward, but He is not there; and backward, but I cannot perceive Him; on the left hand, where He doth work, but I cannot behold Him; He hideth Himself on the right hand, and I see Him not."

How different is this failure to realize the presence of God to the blessed experience of His nearness realized by some.

Brother Lawrence, the simple-minded cook, tells us that for more than sixty years he never lost the sense of the presence of God, but was as conscious of it while performing the duties of his humble office, as when partaking of the Holy Supper.

John Howe, on the blank page of his Bible, made this record in Latin: "This very morning I awoke out of a most ravishing and delightful dream, when a wonderful and copious stream of celestial rays, from the lofty throne of the Divine Majesty, seemed to dart into my open and expanded breast. I have often since reflected on that very signal pledge of special Divine favor, and have with repeated fresh pleasure tasted the delights thereof."

Another experience is recorded thus: "Suddenly there came on my soul a something I had never known before. It was as if some One Infinite and Almighty, knowing everything, full of the deepest, tenderest interest in myself, made known to me that He loved me. My eye saw no one, but I knew assuredly that the One whom I knew not, and had never met, had met me for the first time, and made known to me that we were together."

Are not these experiences so blessed and inspiring, similar to that of the author of the longest, and, in some respects, the sublimest Psalm in the Psalter? He had been beating out the golden ore of thought through successive paragraphs of marvelous power and beauty, when suddenly he seems to have become conscious that He, of whom he had been speaking, had drawn near, and was bending over him. The sense of the presence of God was borne in upon his inner consciousness. And, lifting up a face, on which reverence and ecstasy met and mingled, he cried, *"Thou art near, Lord!"* (cxix. 151).

If only such an experience of the nearness of God were always ours, enwrapping us as air or light; if only we could feel, as the great Apostle put it on Mars' Hill, that God is not far away, but the element in which we have our being, as sea-flowers in deep still lagoons; — then we should understand what David meant when he spoke about dwelling in the house of the Lord all the days of his life, beholding His beauty, inquiring in His temple, and hidden in the secret of His pavilion (Ps. xxvii.). Then, too, we should acquire the blessed secret of *peace, purity,* and *power.*

In the Secret of His Presence there is Peace. "In the world ye shall have tribulation," our Master said, "but in Me ye shall have peace." It is said that a certain insect has the power of surrounding itself with a film of air, encompassed in which it drops into the midst of muddy, stagnant pools, and remains unhurt. And the believer is also conscious that he is enclosed in the invisible film of the Divine Presence, as a far-traveled letter in the envelope which protects it from hurt and soil.

"They draw near me that follow after mischief," but Thou art nearer than the nearest, and I dwell in the inner ring of Thy presence; the mountains round about me are filled with the horses and chariots of Thy protection; no weapon that is formed against me can prosper, for it can only reach me through Thee, and, touching Thee, will glance harmlessly aside. To be in God is to be in a well-fitted house when the storm has slipped from its leash; or in a sanctuary, the doors of which shut out the pursuer.

In the Secret of His Presence there is Purity. The mere vision of snow-capped Alps, seen from afar across Geneva's lake, so elevates and transfigures the rapt and wistful soul as to abash all evil things which would thrust themselves upon the inner life. The presence of a little child, with its guileless purity, has been known to disarm passion, as a beam of light, falling in a reptile-haunted cave, scatters the slimy snakes. But what shall not Thy presence do for me, if I acquire a perpetual sense of it, and live in its secret place? Surely, in the heart of that fire, black cinder though I be, I shall be kept pure, and glowing, and intense!

In the Secret of His Presence there is Power. My cry, day and night, is for power — spiritual power. Not the power of intellect, oratory, or human might. These cannot avail to vanquish the serried ranks of evil. Thou sayest truly that it is not by might or power. Yet human souls which touch Thee become magnetized, and charged with a spiritual force which the world can neither gainsay nor resist. Oh! let me touch Thee! Let me dwell in unbroken contact with Thee, that out of Thee successive tides of Divine energy may pass into and through my emptied and eager spirit, flowing, but never ebbing, and lifting me into a life of blessed ministry, which shall make deserts like the garden of the Lord.

But how shall we get and keep this sense of God's nearness? Must we go back to Bethel, with its pillar of stone, where even Jacob said, "Surely God is in this place?" Ah, we might have stood beside him, with unanointed eye, and seen no ladder, heard no voice; whilst the patriarch would discover God in the bare moorlands of our lives, trodden by us without reverence or joy. Must we travel to the mouth of the cave in whose shadow *Elijah* stood, thrilled by the music of the still small voice, sweeter by contrast with the thunder and the storm? Alas! we might have stood beside him unconscious of that glorious Presence, whilst Elijah, if living now, would discern it in the whisper of the wind, the babbling of babes, the rhythm of heart-throbs. If we had stationed ourselves in our present state beside the *Apostle Paul* when he was caught into the third heaven, we should probably have seen nothing but a tentmaker's shop, or a dingy room in a hired lodging. We in the dark, whilst he was in transports. Whilst he would discern, were he to live again, angels on our steam-ships, visions in our temples, doors opening into heaven amid the tempered glories of our more sombre skies.

In point of fact we carry everywhere our circumference of light or dark. God is as much in the world as He was when Enoch walked with Him, and Moses communed with Him face to face. He is as willing to be a living, bright, glorious Reality to us as to them. But the fault is with us. Our eyes are unanointed, because our hearts are not right. The pure in heart still see God. And to those who love Him, and do His commandments, He still manifests Himself as He does not to the world. Let us cease to blame our times; let us blame ourselves. We are degenerate, not they.

What, then, is that temper of soul which most readily perceives the presence and nearness of God? Let us endeavor to learn the blessed secret of abiding ever in the secret of His Presence and of being hidden in His Pavilion (Ps. xxxi. 20).

Remember then, at the outset, that neither thou, nor any of our race, can have that glad consciousness of the Presence of God except through Jesus. None knoweth the Father but the Son, and those to whom the Son reveals Him; and none cometh to the Father but by Him. Apart from Jesus the Presence of God is an object of terror, from which devils hide themselves in hell, and sinners weave aprons, or hide among the trees. But in Him all barriers are broken down, all veils rent, all clouds dispersed, and the weakest believer may live, where Moses sojourned, in the midst of the fire, before whose consuming flames no impurity can stand.

What part of the Lord's work is most closely connected with this blessed sense of the Presence of God?

It is through the blood of His Cross that sinners are made nigh. For in His death He not only revealed the tender love of God, but put away our sins, and wove for us those garments of stainless beauty, in which we are gladly welcomed into the inner Presence-chamber of the King: Remember it is said: "I will commune with thee from off the mercy-seat." That golden slab on which Aaron sprinkled blood whenever he entered the most Holy Place was a type of Jesus. He is the true mercy-seat. And it is when thou enterest into deepest fellowship with Him in His death, and livest most constantly in the spirit of His memorial supper, that thou shalt realize most deeply His nearness. Now, as at Emmaus, He loves to make Himself known in the breaking of bread.

And is this all? for I have heard this many times, and still fail to live in the secret place as I would.

Exactly so; and therefore, to do for us what no effort of ours could do, our Lord has received of His Father the promise of the Holy Ghost, that He should bring into our hearts the very Presence of God. Understand that since thou art Christ's, the blessed Comforter is thine. He is within thee as He was within thy Lord; and in proportion as thou dost live in the Spirit, and walk in the Spirit, and open thine entire nature to Him, thou wilt find thyself becoming His Presence-chamber, irradiated with the light of His glory. And as thou dost realize that He is in thee, thou wilt realize that thou art ever in Him. Thus the beloved Apostle wrote, "Hereby know we that we dwell in Him, and He in us, because He hath given us of His Spirit."

All this I know, and yet I fail to realize this marvelous fact of the indwelling of the Spirit in me; how then can I ever realize my indwelling in Him?

It is because thy life is so hurried; thou dost not take time enough for meditation and prayer; the Spirit of God within thee and the Presence of God without thee cannot be discerned whilst the senses are occupied with pleasure, or the pulse beats quickly, or the brain is filled with the tread of many hurrying thoughts. It is when water stands that it becomes pellucid, and reveals the pebbly beach below. Be still, and know that God is within thee and around. In the hush of the soul the unseen becomes visible, and the eternal real. The eye dazzled by the sun cannot detect the beauties of its pavilion till it has had time to rid itself of the glare. Let no day pass without its season of silent waiting before God.

Are there any other conditions which I should fulfill, so that I may abide in the secret of His Presence?

"Be pure in heart." Every permitted sin encrusts the windows of the soul with thicker layers of grime, obscuring the vision of God. But every victory over impurity and selfishness clears the spiritual vision, and there fall from the eyes, as it had been, scales. In the power of the Holy Ghost deny self, give no quarter to sin, resist the devil, and thou shalt see God.

The unholy soul could not see God, even though it were set down in the midst of heaven. But holy souls see God amid the ordinary commonplaces of earth, and find everywhere an open vision. Such could not be nearer God, though they stood by the sea of glass. Their only advantage there would be that, the veil of their mortal and sinful natures having been rent, the vision would be directer and more perfect.

Keep His commandments. Let there be not one jot or tittle unrecognized and unkept. *He that hath My commandments and keepeth them, he it is that loveth Me, and he that loveth Me shall he loved of My Father, and I will love him, and will manifest Myself to him,* Moses, the faithful servant, was also the seer, and spake with God face to face as a man speaketh with his friend.

Continue in the Spirit of Prayer. Sometimes the vision will tarry to test the earnestness and steadfastness of thy desire. At other times it will come as the dawn steals over the sky, and, or ever thou art aware thou wilt find thyself conscious that He is near. He was ever wont to glide unheralded, into the midst of His disciples through unopened doors. "Thy footsteps are not known."

At such times we may truly say with St. Bernard: "He entered not by the eyes, for His presence was not marked by color; nor by the ears, for there was no sound; nor by the breath, for He mingled not with the air; nor by the touch, for He was impalpable. You ask, then, how I knew that He was present. Because He was a quickening power. As soon as He entered, He awoke my slumbering soul; He moved and pierced my heart, which before was strange, stony, hard and sick, so that my soul could bless the Lord, and all that is within me praised His Holy Name."

Cultivate the habit of speaking aloud to God. Not, perhaps, always, because our desires are often too sacred or deep to be put into words. But it is well to acquire the habit of speaking to God as to a present friend whilst sitting in the house or walking by the way. Seek the habit of talking things over with God — thy letters, thy plans, thy hopes, thy mistakes, thy sorrows and sins. Things look very differently when brought into the calm light of His presence. One cannot talk long with God aloud without feeling that He is near.

Meditate much upon the Word. This is the garden where the Lord God walks, the temple where He dwells, the presence-chamber where He holds court, and is found by those who seek Him. It is through the word that we feed upon the Word. And He said: "He that eateth My flesh, and drinketh My blood, dwelleth in Me and I in him."

Be diligent in Christian work. The place of prayer is indeed the place of His manifested presence. But that presence would fade from it were we to linger there after the bell of duty had rung for us below. But we shall ever meet it as we go about our necessary work; "Thou meetest him that worketh righteousness." As we go forth to our daily tasks the angel of His presence comes to greet us, and turns to go at our side. "Go ye," said the Master. "Lo I am with you all the days." Not only in temple courts, or in sequestered glens, or in sick rooms, but in the round of daily duty, in the common-places of life, on the dead levels of existence, we may be ever in the secret of His Presence, and shall be able to say with Elijah before Ahab, and Gabriel to Zacharias, "I stand in the presence of God" (1 Kings xvii. 1; Luke i. 19).

Let us cultivate the habit of recognizing the Presence of God. "Blessed is the man whom Thou choosest, and causest to approach unto Thee, that He may dwell in Thy courts." There is no life like this. To feel that God is with us. That He never leads us through a place too narrow for Him to pass as well. That we can never be lonely again, never for a single moment. That we are beset by Him behind and before, and covered by His hand. That He could not be nearer to us, even if we were in heaven itself. To have Him as Friend, and Referee, and Counsellor, and Guide. To realize that there is never to be a Jericho in our lives without the presence of the Captain of the Lord's host, with those invisible but mighty legions, before whose charge all walls must fall down. What wonder that the saints of old waxed valiant in fight as they heard Him say: "I am with thee; I will never leave nor forsake thee." Begone fear and sorrow and dread of the dark valley! "Thou shalt hide me in the secret of Thy Presence from the pride of man; Thou shalt keep me secretly in a pavilion from the strife of tongues."

The Secret of Christ's Indwelling

IT is meet that the largest church in the greatest Gentile city in the world should be dedicated to the Apostle Paul, for Gentiles are under a great obligation to him as the Apostle of the Gentiles. It is to him that we owe, under the Spirit of God, the unveiling of two great mysteries, which specially touch us as Gentiles.

The *first* of these, glorious as it is, we cannot now stay to discuss, though it wrought a revolution when first preached and maintained by the Apostle in the face of the most strenuous opposition. Till then. Gentiles were expected to become Jews before they were Christians, and to pass through the synagogue to the church. But he showed that this was not needful, and that Gentiles stood on the same level as Jews with respect to the privileges of the gospel — fellow-heirs and fellow-members of the body, and fellow-partakers of the promise in Christ Jesus through the gospel (Eph. iii. 6).

The *second,* however, well deserves our further thought, for if only it could be realized by the children of God, they would begin to live after so Divine a fashion as to still the enemy and avenger, and to repeat in some small measure the life of Jesus on the earth.

This mystery is *that the Lord Jesus is willing to dwell within the Gentile heart.* That He should dwell in the heart of a child of Abraham was deemed a marvelous act of condescension; but that He should find a home in the heart of a Gentile was incredible. This mistake was, however, dissipated before the radiant revelation of truth made to him who, in his own judgment, was not meet to be called an Apostle, because he had persecuted the Church of God. God was pleased to make known through him "the riches of the glory of this mystery among the Gentiles; which is Christ in you, the hope of glory" (Col. 1.27).

"Master, where dwellest Thou?" they asked of old. And in reply Jesus led them from the crowded Jordan bank to the slight tabernacle of woven osiers where He temporarily lodged. But if we address the same question to Him now, He will point, not to the high and lofty dome of heaven, not to the splendid structure of stone or marble, but to the happy spirit that loves, trusts, and obeys Him. "Behold," saith He, "I stand at the door and knock. If any man hear My voice, and open the door, I will come in to him." "We will come," He said, including His Father with Himself, "and make our abode with him." He promised to be within each believer as a tenant in a house; as sap in the branch; as life-blood and life-energy in each member, however feeble, of the body.

I. — **The Mystery.** Christ is in the believer. He indwells the heart by faith, as the sun indwells the lowliest flowers that unfurl their petals and bare their hearts to his beams. Not because we are good. Not because we are trying to be whole-hearted in our consecration. Not because we keep Him by the te-

26

nacity of our love. But because we believe, and, in believing, have thrown open all the doors and windows of our nature. And He has come in.

He probably came in so quietly that we failed to detect His entrance. There was no footfall along the passage; the chime of the golden bells at the foot of His priestly robe did not betray Him; He stole in on the wing of the morning, or like the noiselessness with which nature arises from her winter's sleep and arrays herself in the robes which her Creator has prepared for her. But this is the way of Christ. He does not strive, nor cry, nor lift up or cause His voice to be heard. His tread is so light that it does not break bruised reeds, His breath so soft that it can re-illumine dying sparks. Do not be surprised, therefore, if you cannot tell the day or the hour when the Son of Man came to dwell within you. Only know that He has come. "Know ye not as to your own selves, that Jesus Christ is in you? unless ye be reprobate" (2 Cor. xiii. 5).

It is very wonderful. Yes; the heavens, even the heavens of heavens, with all their light and glory, alone seem worthy of Him. But even there He is not more at home than He is with the humble and contrite spirit that simply trusts in Him. In His earthly life He said that the Father dwelt in Him so really that the words He spake and the works He did were not His own, but His Father's. And He desires to be in us as His Father was in Him, so that the outgoings of our life may be channels through which He, hidden within, may pour Himself forth upon men.

It is not generally recognized. It is not; though that does not disprove it. We fail to recognize many things in ourselves and in nature around, which are nevertheless true. But there is a reason why many whose natures are certainly the temple of Christ, remain ignorant of the presence of the wonderful Tenant that sojourns within. *He dwells so deep.* Below the life of the body, which is as the curtain of the tent; below the life of the soul, where thought and feeling, judgment and imagination, hope and love, go to and fro, ministering as white-stoled priests in the holy place; below the play of light and shade, resolution and will, memory and hope, the perpetual ebb and flow of the tides of self-consciousness, there, through the Holy Spirit, Christ dwells, as of old the Shechinah dwelt in the Most Holy Place, closely shrouded from the view of man.

It is comparatively seldom that we go into these deeper departments of our being. We are content to live the superficial life of sense. We eat, we drink, we sleep; we give ourselves to enjoy the lust of the flesh, the lust of the eyes, and the pride of life; we fulfill the desires of the flesh and of the mind. Or we abandon ourselves to the pursuit of knowledge and culture, of science and art; we reason, speculate, argue; we make short incursions into the realm of morals, that sense of right and wrong which is part of the make-up of men. But we have too slight an acquaintance with the deeper and more mysterious chamber of the spirit. Now this is why the majority of believers are so insensible of their Divine and wonderful Resident, who makes the regenerated spirit His abode.

27

It is to be accepted by faith. We repeat here our constant mistake about the things of God. We try to feel them. If we feel them, we believe them; otherwise we take no account of them. We reverse the Divine order. We say, *feeling,* faith, FACT. God says, FACT, faith, *feeling.* With Him feeling is of small account — He only asks us to be willing to accept His own Word, and to cling to it because He has spoken it, in entire disregard of what we may feel.

I am distinctly told that Christ, though He is on the Throne in His ascended glory, is also within me by the Holy Ghost. I confess I do not feel him there. Often amid the assault of temptation or the fury of the storm that sweeps over the surface of my nature, I cannot detect His form or hear Him say, "It is I." But I dare to believe He is there: not without me, but within; not as a transient sojourner for a night, but as a perpetual inmate: not altered by my changes from earnestness to lethargy, from the summer of love to the winter of despondency, but always and unchangeably the same. And I say again and again, "Jesus, Thou art here. I am not worthy that Thou shouldest abide under my roof; but Thou hast come. Assert Thyself. Put down all rule, and authority, and power. Come out of Thy secret chamber, and possess all that is within me, that it may bless Thy holy name."

Catherine of Siena at one time spent three days in a solitary retreat, praying for a greater fullness and joy of the Divine presence. Instead of this, it seemed as though legions of wicked spirits assailed her with blasphemous thoughts and evil suggestions. At length, a great light appeared to descend from above. The devils fled, and the Lord Jesus conversed with her. Catherine asked Him, "Lord, where wert Thou when my heart was so tormented?" "I was in thy heart," He answered. "O Lord, Thou art everlasting truth," she replied, "and I humbly bow before Thy word; but how can I believe that Thou wast in my heart when it was filled with such detestable thoughts?" "Did these thoughts give thee pleasure or pain?" He asked. "An exceeding pain and sadness," was her reply. To whom the Lord said, "Thou wast in woe and sadness because I was in the midst of thy heart. My presence it was which rendered those thoughts insupportable to thee. When the period I had determined for the duration of the combat had elapsed, I sent forth the beams of My light, and the shades of hell were dispelled, because they cannot resist that light."

II. — The Glory of this Mystery. When God's secrets break open they do so in glory. The wealth of the root hidden in the ground is revealed in the hues of orchid or scent of rose. The hidden beauty of a beam of light is unraveled in the sevenfold color of the rainbow. The swarming, infinitesimal life of Southern seas breaks into waves of phosphorescence when cleft by the keel of the ship. And whenever the unseen world has revealed itself to mortal eyes it has been in glory. It was especially so at the Transfiguration, when the Lord's nature broke from the strong restraint within which He confined it and revealed itself to the eye of man. "His face did shine as the sun, and His garments became white as the light."

So when we accept the fact of His existence within us deeper than our own, and make it one of the aims of our life to draw on it and develop it, we shall be conscious of a glory transfiguring our life and irradiating ordinary things, such as will make earth, with its commonest engagements, like as the vestibule of heaven.

The wife of Jonathan Edwards had been the subject of great fluctuations in religious experience and frequent depression, till she came to the point of renouncing the world, and yielding herself up to be possessed by these mighty truths. But so soon as this was the case, a marvelous change took place. She began to experience a constant, uninterrupted rest; sweet peace and serenity of soul; a continual rejoicing in all the works of God's hands, whether of nature or of daily providence; a wonderful access to God by prayer, as it were seeing Him and immediately conversing with Him; all tears wiped away; all former troubles and sorrows of life forgotten, excepting grief for past sins and for the dishonor done to Christ in the world; a daily sensible doing and suffering everything for God, and doing all with a continual uninterrupted cheerfulness, peace, and joy.

Such glory — the certain pledge of the glory to be revealed — is within reach of each reader of these lines who will dare day by day to reckon that Christ lives within, and will be content to die to the energies and promptings of the self-life so that there may be room for the Christ-life to reveal itself. "I have been crucified," said the greatest human teacher of this Divine art; "Christ liveth in me; I live by faith in the Son of God."

III. — The Riches of the Glory of this Mystery. When this mystery, or secret, of the Divine life in man is apprehended and made use of, it gives great wealth to life. If all the treasures of wisdom, knowledge, power, and grace reside in Jesus, and He is become the cherished and honored resident of our nature, it is clear that we also must be greatly enriched. It is like a poor man having a millionaire friend come to live with him.

There are riches of patience. Life is not easy to any of us. No branch escapes the pruning -knife; no jewel the wheel; no child the rod. People tyrannize over and vex us almost beyond endurance; circumstances strain us till the chords of our hearts threaten to snap; our nervous system is overtaxed by the rush and competition of our times. Indeed, we have need of patience!

Never to relax the self-watch; never to indulge in unkind or thoughtless criticism of others; never to utter the hasty word, or permit the sharp retort; never to complain, except to God; never to permit hard and distrustful thoughts to lodge within the soul; to be always more thoughtful of others than of self; to detect the one blue spot in the clouded sky; to be on the alert to find an excuse for those who are froward and awkward; to suffer the aches and pains, the privations and trials of life, sweetly, submissively, trustfully; to drink the bitter cup, with the eye fixed on the Father's face, without a murmur or complaint; this needs patience, which mere stoicism could never give.

And we cannot live such a life till we have learnt to avail ourselves of the riches of the indwelling Christ. The beloved Apostle speaks of being a partaker of the patience which is in Jesus (Rev. i. 9). So may we be. That calm, unmurmuring, unreviling patience, which made the Lamb of God dumb before His shearers, is ours. Robert Hall was once overheard saying, amid the heat of an argument, "Calm me, O Lamb of God!" But we may go further, and say, "Lord Jesus, let Thy patience arise in me, as a spring of fresh water in a briny sea."

There are riches of grace. Alone among the great cities of the world, Jerusalem had no river. But the glorious Lord was in the midst of her, and He became a place of broad rivers and streams, supplying from Himself all that rivers gave to cities, at the foot of whose walls the welcome waters lapped (Isa. xxxiii. 21).

This is a picture of what we have, who dare to reckon on the indwelling of "our glorious Lord," as King, Lawgiver, and Saviour. He makes all grace to abound towards us, so that we have a sufficiency for all emergencies, and can abound in every good work. In His strength, ever rising up within us, we are able to do as much as those who are dowered with the greatest mental and natural gifts, and we escape the temptations to vainglory and pride by which they are beset.

The grace of purity and self-control, of fervent prayer and understanding in the Scriptures, of love for men and zeal for God, of lowliness and meekness, of gentleness and goodness — all is in Christ; and if Christ is in us, all is ours also. Oh that we would dare to believe it, and draw on it, letting down the pitcher of faith into the deep well of Christ's indwelling opened within us by the Holy Ghost!

It is impossible, in these brief limits, to elaborate further this wonderful thought. But if only we would meet every call, difficulty, and trial, *not* saying, as we so often do, "I shall never be able to go through it," but saying, "I cannot; but Christ is in me, and He can," we should find that all trials were intended to reveal and unfold the wealth hidden within us, until Christ was literally formed within us, and His life manifested in our mortal body (2 Cor. iv. 10).

(1) Be still each day for a short time, sitting before God in meditation, and ask the Holy Spirit to reveal to you the truth of Christ's indwelling. Ask God to be pleased to make known to *you* what is the riches of the glory of this mystery (Col. i. 27).

(2) Reverence your nature as the temple of the indwelling Lord. As the Eastern unbares his feet, and the Western his head, on entering the precincts of a temple, so be very careful of aught that would defile the body or soil the soul. No beasts must herd in the temple courts. Get Christ to drive them out. "Know ye not that ye are a temple of God? The temple of God is holy, and such are ye."

(3) Hate your own life. "If any man hateth not his own life," said our Lord, "he cannot be My disciple" (Luke xiv. 26). And the word translated "life" is *soul*, the seat and center of the self-life with its restless energies and activities, its choices and decisions, its ceaseless strivings and independence and leadership. This is the greatest hindrance to our enjoyment of the indwelling Christ. If we will acquire the habit of saying "No," not only to our bad but our good self; if we will daily deliver ourselves up to death for Jesus' sake; if we will take up our cross and follow the Master, though it be to His grave, we shall become increasingly conscious of being possessed by a richer, deeper, Diviner life than our own.

With Christ in Separation

THE Bible rings with the cry for separation. Those words, *Divide! Divide!* so often heard in the House of Commons, compelling every man to take a side, speak through its pages, from those earliest verses which tell how God divided the light from the darkness.

This call came to Abraham, bidding him get out from country and kindred and father's house; to Moses as the bugle-note of the Exodus; to the tribe of Levi, mustering them at the gate of the camp; to the children of Israel, as they languished in Babylon, bidding them return to their fatherland; and along the resounding aisles of the New Testament Church, these words re-echo: "Come out from among them, and be ye separate, saith the Lord, and touch not the unclean thing; and I will receive you, and will be a Father unto you;" "Come out of her, My people, that ye be not partakers of her sins, and that ye receive not of her plagues" (2 Cor. vi. 17, and Rev. xviii. 4).

But what is that separation to WHICH WE ARE CALLED? There are many counterfeits, against which we do well to be on our guard. *It is not the separation of the monk*. This has ever fascinated noble minds. For like-minded men to go off together to some sequestered vale, protected from the storms that sweep across the world; to build for themselves homes and temples, and mingle their toils with holy meditation and prayer; welcoming the daybreak with matins, and greeting with vesper hymns the first couriers of the starry host; such was the dream that stirred the imagination of saintly hearts in the Middle Ages. And something like this filled the *Mayflower* with the Pilgrim Fathers, and peopled the Black Forest with colonies of Moravian settlers.

But such separation, however attractive, cannot be the separation of Christ. He solemnly prayed that we might not be taken out of the world; yea, He expressly sent us into the world. And what would become of it if we were all to withdraw from its life? Night without a star; a rock-bound coast without a lighthouse beam raying out into the murky gloom; a vessel drifting on the rocks without a watch on deck; a carcase corrupting in midsummer without salt! No, this cannot be the separation to which we are called.

It is not the separation of the Pharisee. The Pharisees held that a man could be religious without being good. He might be full of extortion and excess, if only he washed the outside of cup and platter; full of dead men's bones, if only he appeared clean as a white-washed sepulchre. In their judgment, therefore, impurity was not a matter of inward evil, but communicated by a touch. To be touched by a man who had not washed since eating would be sufficient to defile the stately Pharisee.

But our Lord forever broke down these unrighteous distinctions. He taught not only by speech, but by action, that impurity is not communicated by contact, but is nurtured in the heart, and bred in act and speech. He did not wash after His meals; He ate with publicans and sinners; He let a fallen woman weep at His feet; He touched the bleared eye of blindness, the tied tongue of dumbness, the polluted flesh of the leper. Repeatedly we are told that He stretched forth His hand and touched.

And is not this what the world wants? It needs hand-help — the touch of the King. We shall never be able to help men by simply looking on them or exhorting them; we must *touch* them. Those lily-white delicate jeweled hands which may turn this page must be yielded to Christ, that He may use them and work through them His miracles of mercy in our weary age. And such contact will not defile. Pitch is a disinfectant; so far from defiling, it will tend to promote our love for purity, when we dare the contact, in the name of Christ and for the welfare of a dying world.

It is not the separation of the Stoic. The Puritans were not entirely free from this mistake. For them the world was a great howling wilderness; laughter and mirth signs of an unregenerate soul; their scheme of life too narrow and severe to admit of those lighter and softer passages which relieve its strain and draw out the tenderer sentiments of human hearts.

Against this, Christ's life was a perpetual protest. He mingled with wedding guests, smiled at the children as they played in the market-places and called to their fellows, directed the crowds to the beauties of the flowers and the habits of the birds, noticed the sunrise hues and evening tints, and lived as a man amongst men. However severe He might be to the formalists of His time. He had ever a warm heart towards what was natural and human. Let us not forget the command, T*hou shall rejoice in every good thing which the Lord thy God giveth thee,* and let us cultivate the habit of extracting joy and blessing from all the innocent and beautiful things around us.

The necessity of answering this Question is really urgent. It is a *pressing* question. Hundreds of young Christians are asking what they should do or avoid; and in so many cases, for want of a clear principle, begin to drift; the bloom passes off the basket of summer fruit, and when once gone, can never be replaced. It is a *pertinent* question, especially at those seasons of the year when the dark evenings afford such abundant opportunities for the dance, the ball, the theatre, and the opera. It is also a *perplexing* question, because good people are found on such opposite sides, and give answers, wide as the poles asunder, to the various questions with which they are plied. Some forbid the theatre, but allow the opera. Some have no objection to the children's pantomime, but are horrified at the proposal to see an ordinary play. Some would go to see Shakespearean plays, but would not go to others. Some distinguish between a dance and a ball.

What is the result? Christian ministers frequent theatres. Professors give dancing-parties not far removed from balls. Funds for religious purposes are raised by private theatricals. Our young people are perpetually loosening the restraints by which they are held, pressing outwards the fences which divide them from the world, taking in new lengths of territory, and fretting against restraint.

Are there no self-acting principles, so that each individual soul may decide for itself these difficult, doubtful, and perilous problems which are so incessantly cropping up in all lives, either in one form or another? There are, and the following are surely amongst them; and, like the spear of the seraph Ithuriel, will indicate by a touch the evil that may lurk under innocent appearances: —

1. — *Beware of everything which is Inconsistent with your Relationship to the Lord Jesus.* What is that relationship? And, of course, we are dealing here with the case of those alone who are His, or who are desirous of being identified with Him, both here and hereafter.

We are His servants; bought by His blood, sworn to loyal allegiance. Is it quite consistent, then, to be mingling with the amusements and gaieties of the world, which is of the same spirit to-day as when it cast Him out of its camp and crucified Him? It has an ugly look about it when loyal soldiers fraternize in the carousals of rebels.

We are His members; bone of His bone, flesh of His flesh, whom He nourishes and cherishes. Our Head is already passed through the grave on to resurrection-ground, where He is gathering around Him His own — His kindred. Is it not incongruous for the Head to be on one side of the grave and the members on the other? Is it not altogether unbecoming to pretend to be one with Him in His risen glory, whilst we are practically as close as we dare in our contact with the world which He has left?

We are His Bride; He, the Heavenly Bridegroom, is one with us in a union which has no analogy, save that of wedlock, where heart locks with heart. Is it consistent with fidelity to Him for us to dally with the world, whose hands were imbued with His blood? What did the people of Scotland think of the familiarities of marriage between Mary Queen of Scots and Both well, the murderer of her first husband, Darnley?

Surely the Cross, with outstretched arms, bars the bridge between us and the world; and we may cry with the Apostle, "Far be it from me to glory, save in the Cross of our Lord Jesus Christ, through which the world has been crucified unto me, and I unto the world."

Whenever, then, there is any doubt as to whether it be right to go to this place or that, bring the question beneath the light that streams from the Cross and from the Throne; clear your heart and mind of all selfish aims and thoughts of what others may do or say; let your eye be single to discern the will of the Lord; ask what He would have you to do; and before long the difficulties will roll up as quickly and noiselessly as the mists which fill the mountain valleys before the touch of the summer sun; your whole body will be full of light; you will even lose your taste for the things which once you loved; and in the new-found ecstasy of the Living Water, welling up in your heart, you will be prepared to leave behind the water-pot on which you had been relying as the source of your life.

2. — *Beware of anything which the world itself would deem inconsistent.* Though the world is not religious in our sense, yet it has a very keen appreciation of true Christianity, and a very high ideal of what Christians should be. And we may well arrest our steps when we are met with a surprised interrogation — "What! are you here? We didn't expect to see you!" The very fuss which is made over us when we step over the line may well make us pause and ask whether we have not done something to forfeit the smile and "Well done" of Jesus.

3. — *Beware of anything which would injure some weaker conscience.* This is one of the most important considerations in Christian living. "All things are lawful to me, but all things are not expedient." And why are they not expedient? It is inexpedient to do things which may be harmless enough in themselves, and which you may feel able to do with impunity, if in doing them you lead others to do them also, not because they feel a.t ease, but simply because they are emboldened by your example, regarding you as further advanced than themselves in the Christian life, and therefore a trustworthy guide. Estimate every action, not only as it is in itself, but as it is likely to be in its influence on others, lest you break down wholesome barriers, and place them in scenes of temptation which, however, harmless to yourself, are perilous in the extreme to them. We have no right to lead our young children up perilous passes, where we may clamber with clear head and nimble foot, but where *their* inexperienced steps may slide into the abyss.

4. — *Beware of scenes and companionships which dull your spiritual life.* Who is there that does not long for a life on fire? But how can we possibly look for such a thing if we are persistently exposing ourselves to influences which choke and repress it and damp it down? There are some scenes which seem incompatible with earnest prayer and Bible study, ere we retire to rest; which lower the inner temperature; which! leave an ill-flavor in the mouth; which poison the young life, as the noxious gas-fumes poison the life of flowers and plants. From all such scenes we do well to refrain our feet.

5. — *Beware of any society in which you feel compelled to put a bushel over your testimony.* We must shine as lights in the world. And the most necessary condition in a lighthouse lamp is its permanence. If it shines at one time, and

is hidden at another, now flashing afar over the dark seething waves, and then standing somber and obscure on the beetling cliffs, of what use is it? It is worse than useless. And if we are to be of any real use in this world, our testimony for Jesus must be maintained, in season and out of season, in storm and sunshine, always and everywhere. But if, before going into any scene or fellowship, you have to remind yourself that you must not touch on any of those subjects which are dearest to your soul, you may well fear lest you are trespassing on forbidden ground. *Go nowhere that you cannot take Jesus with you, and ask His blessing before going.* "*Do all in the glory of God.*"

All this will involve a hard fight, persecution, and misunderstanding. It is thus, however, that we prove our lineage with the noble martyr-spirits of the past. See that young girl, in the days of Diocletian, beautiful and richly dressed, standing before the altar, with the judge on the one side, her lover on the other, her companions grouped around. If she will but throw a few grains of incense on the brazier she shall be spared from cruel death and given back to love and friends and life. But not a grain is cast upon the expectant flames, and she is ruthlessly led off to die for Him whom she loves better than all. Was she not consistent? Would you not have done the same? Then do the same now, and dare to be consistent to your lover, Christ.

Sometimes we may be placed in such a position, that we have no alternative than to go into scenes which, for ourselves, we would not choose. For instance, when the worldly mother of a Christian girl insists on her accompanying her into society, where there is nothing positively sinful, but much that is light and thoughtless, it would evidently be her duty to go. You may ask to be excused, but if your plea is not allowed, you must go, unless conscience positively forbids, and Christ will go with you, keeping your heart.

There are many Compensations. This is the only *safe* course. The world is so attractive, and so appeals to our weaknesses, that if we once launch upon its waters, they will insensibly sweep us toward the rush of the whirlpool, and we shall go down into the deep, dark abyss. It is the only *strong* course. He who would lift me must stand above me. Who did most for Sodom: Lot who went down into it and sat in the gate, or Abraham who got up early to the place where he stood before the Lord? The old heathen games were swept off the world, not because the early Christians went to them, but because they stopped away. The brutal sports of the last century fled away, not because the Methodists patronized them, but because they abstained from them. And the moral pests of modern society will never succumb until good people withdraw both their patronage and support. This is the only *blessed* course, because God's promise of being a Father and of receiving us is entirely dependent on our complying with His conditions. It is when father and mother forsake that the Lord gathers us; when the synagogue casts us out that Jesus finds us; when heart and flesh fail that He is the strength of our heart and our portion forever.

Dare to go outside the camp, at the risk of being counted singular and unfriendly! Let the world treat you as it did your Lord. Why should the servant be fawned on and flattered where the Master was crucified as a felon? Lie in His grave, and thus you shall know the joy of His Easter life, the sweetness of His love, and the closeness of His friendship, which would compensate for a thousand deaths. To know the King you must share His exile.

Gather ye, gather ye, out to the lone Cave of Adullam, and around the standard of the exiled Prince; and when He comes again in triumph to be crowned with the diadem of universal empire, ye shall appear in His train and by His side, confessed and acknowledged as those of whom He has no reason to be ashamed.

The Filling of the Holy Spirit

COMING suddenly down to Ephesus, the Apostle Paul, as was his wont, sought for any Christians that might be gathered within that vast center of heathenism. His search was finally rewarded by the discovery of twelve men, meeting probably in some obscure room, and exercising no influence on the vast idolatrous city out of which the grace of God had drawn them. His first question was a very searching one. Without preliminaries he went to the point. Convinced that there must be some reason why they did not exercise a greater power on the populations around them, he set himself to probe the cause; and shrewdly guessed it in the searching inquiry: "Did ye receive the Holy Spirit when ye believed?" (Acts xix. 2, R. V.).

The Apostle surely did not mean to ask whether they had received the special gifts of the Spirit. Their reply at least does not indicate that they so understood him. He wanted only to learn whether they had received that filling of the Holy Spirit which was the main feature of Pentecost (Acts ii. 4, vi. 3, xiii. 52).

"Received we the Holy Spirit when we believed! How could we have faith, except it were given us by the Holy Spirit?" might have been the reply of the startled men. "Granted," would the Apostle answer. "No man can call Jesus Lord except by the Holy Spirit; certainly the Holy Spirit has been at work within you, else ye were none of Christ's; but there is an experience altogether beyond and above that initial step by which the Holy Spirit first reveals sin and Christ, and it is for lack of this that your testimony is so inoperative, and your lives so destitute of fire."

And as we look back upon this episode across the centuries, we are convinced that it suggests the reason why so many Christians around us acknowledge their religion a failure, whilst the world mocks at their inability to exercise the devils which possess it.

It is of course true that the Holy Ghost is the sole agent in conversion, becoming the occupant of the temple, which is presented to Him by the nature of man (1 Cor. vi. 19). And it is equally clear, that the Holy Spirit as a person enters the newly regenerated heart. But there is a vast difference between having the Holy Ghost and being filled by Him. In the one case, He may be compared to a mighty man that cannot save, relegated to an obscure corner of the heart, whilst the larger part of the nature is excluded from His gracious influences. In the other, He is a welcome guest, to whom every part of the being is thrown open, and who pervades it with the freedom of the balmy air of summer, sweeping through open windows, breathing through long corridors, and carrying into further recesses the fragrance of a thousand flowers.

There are a great many Christians who undoubtedly received the Holy Spirit at the earliest moment of faith; indeed, their faith is the result of His work; but they have never gone further; they have never yielded their whole nature to His indwelling; they have had no further experience of His Pentecostal Filling.

It is not difficult to point this contrast by analogies drawn from the Word of God. May we not reverently say that the ministry of our blessed Lord Himself owed much of its marvelous power to that moment when, although filled with the Holy Spirit from His birth. He was afresh anointed at the waters of baptism? With marked emphasis it is said He was filled with the Spirit (Luke iv. 1), and returned in the power of the Spirit unto Galilee (ver. 14), and stood up in the synagogue of His native town, claiming the ancient prophecy, and declaring that the Spirit of God was upon Him (ver. 18). His wondrous words and works are directly traced to the marvelous operation of the Holy Ghost upon His human life (Acts x. 38).

Remember also the vast alteration that came over the Apostles and other followers of Jesus Christ on the Day of Pentecost and after! Before that day, they cowered like sheep; when it came, they stood like lions at bay. Before it, their bosoms heaved with tumultuous passions of rivalry and suspicion and desire for earthly power; afterwards, each thought the other better than himself, and sought to excel in humble ministry to the saints. Peter charged home upon the crowd the murder of the Son of God, until the rabble became a congregation, and thousands cried for mercy. Can you recognize in him the timid son of Jonas who dared not face the question of a servant-girl? And what made the difference? From the first they had enjoyed the teaching and grace of the Holy Spirit. Though not given in fullness (John vii. 39), yet He was working on human hearts (Luke ii. 25-27). Indeed, our Lord had breathed on them and said, "Receive ye the Holy Ghost" (John xx. 22), before He went on to say, "Ye shall be baptized with the Holy Ghost not many days hence." What does this mean, except that those who have already received the Spirit, in a lower measure, may look for and receive His gracious filling — grace on grace, wave on wave, flood on flood?

The same truth is taught by contrast between Romans vii., an arid wilderness, marked by one or two green spots, and Romans viii., a very garden of the Lord, full of murmuring streams from Lebanon, bringing fertility and beauty into all hearts, lives, homes, and churches where they come. The one chapter describes a life which lacks the fullness of the Spirit, the other rings from end to end with mention of His person, offices, and work.

Reader, can you not see here the reason of the failure and disappointment of your life? You are living experimentally on the other side of Pentecost. The Holy Ghost is in you, but He does not fill you. You are trying to live a Christian life in the neglect of the one power by which this marvel can be achieved. What wonder that you fail, and are often inclined to give up in despair, because your ideal is so far beyond your reach; or that your closest friends sadly contrast the luxuriance of your promises with the meagerness of your fruit? It is hardly necessary to ask if you received the filling of the Holy Spirit when you believed. It is but too patent that you did not; and if in this hour of unusual thoughtfulness you were led to see your position, and seek that holy filling which you may have, there is not the least doubt that you would suddenly rise up into an excellency of Christian living which would be as great a contrast to your past as sunlight to moonlight, and as the profusion of an autumn orchard to the bare and storm-swept trees of winter.

This is the glorious meaning of the day of Pentecost; it has put within the reach of all, of old men and children, of young men and maidens, that blessed filling of the Spirit which in former times was reserved for only a few of the most illustrious saints (Acts ii. 17-18).

Mark these several ways in which this filling of the Spirit would operate, 1. — *You would get a new and vivid conception of the Lord Jesus.* Is it not your chief complaint that His figure is so indistinct, and that you are so unable to realize His presence; the glimpses of His face few and far between, and your moments of true communion fitful? The reason is to be found in the feebleness of the Spirit's action. It is His special function to take of the things of Christ, and to reveal them to us, and one chief symptom of His having filled the soul is that the soul luxuriates in a vivid and abiding recognition of the Lord's real and glorious presence. Nay, more, Christ dwells in us by the Holy Spirit, as the sun dwells in the world by the atmosphere vibrating in his beams (Eph. iii. 17).

2. — *You would obtain more constant victory over sin.* How many Christians complain of the uprisings of their old and depraved nature, which so rapidly responds to the suggestions of the tempter, betraying the continued presence in the heart of that self-principle which has been the cause of all the evil and misery of the world! To cope with this is the enigma of many hearts, ambitious of saintliness; and of how many is it the bitter regret that length of years and experience and incessant struggles, fail to give them victory! This also is largely because there has been no deep experience of the filling of the Holy Spirit.

It is His special work to deal with these uprisings. Without Him they laugh us to scorn, as the tumultuous waves the injunction of Canute; but let Him occupy the heart in his Divine glory, and He lusts against the flesh, so that we may not do the things we would (Gal. v. 17). The law of the Spirit of life in Christ Jesus makes us free from the law of sin and death which is in our members (Rom. viii. 2). There is no greater safeguard against impurity and sin, than to reckon that the whole nature has now become the Temple of the Holy Spirit, and to trust Him to keep His own property absolutely for Himself (i Cor. vi. 19).

3. — *You would have a more unbroken assurance of acceptance and adoption into the family of God.* To ignore or lessen the work of the Spirit in the heart is to silence the one voice which witnesses with our spirits that we are born of God (Rom. viii. 15). What does the Apostle mean when he says, "After that ye believed ye were sealed with that holy Spirit of promise, which is the earnest of our inheritance?" Those words surely teach us that what the earnest penny is to the farm-laborer, what the first sod to the purchaser of Scotch estates, what the grapes of Eschol to the vintage of Palestine, of which they are the guarantee and the sample, — that the presence of the Holy Spirit in the believer's heart is to the glorious inheritance reserved for us in heaven. It stands to reason, therefore, that the strength and clearness of His witness will be in proportion to the fullness of His indwelling. Let us do everything to increase and accentuate the power of this precious testimony to our childship.

4. — *You would obtain new power for service.* It is said, that when the Apostles had prayed, the place where they met was shaken, "and they were all filled with the Holy Ghost, and spake the Word of God with boldness, and with great power gave they witness" (Acts iv. 31-33). Little enough power may have rested upon your work for God. You have waved the censer between the living and the dead, and the plague has not stayed. You have spoken the old words that once acted as a charm, but no miracle of grace has followed. You have plied the weary routine of work from year to year, without winning a single soul for the Master. Ah! terrible waste of energy. Much as if a man were to try to turn a ponderous machine by hand instead of attaching it to the fly-wheel of a vast engine revolving rapidly but uselessly within his reach.

The Holy Spirit is a Spirit of power, the dynamics of the kingdom of heaven, the energy of the life of God, which can alone vivify dead spirits. The more we have of this, the more certain we are of great spiritual results; whilst, without this, we may sow much, but our seed will be lost, and the scanty ears of autumn fail to reward our toils. The life-giving Spirit must be with us in power, or we shall never see dead souls awake to the life of God under our word.

5. — *You would be kept in mind of your true attitude in Jesus.* We forget so soon. In the onset of evil we do not recollect to look away to Him. Long periods of time pass during which we are but faintly conscious that we are God's adopted children, sharing the victory of our risen Lord, and destined to stand forever in the inner circle of the Throne. And this is because the Holy Ghost has so little power in our lives; whereas if only we were filled with His in-

dwelling, He would be in us as the Spirit of remembrance, bringing all things to our memory, and keeping us in the true posture of all holy souls (John xiv. 26).

I am not anxious here to distinguish between the filling of the Holy Ghost and the baptism of fire. So far as I can understand it, they are synonymous. In Acts i. 5 our Lord said, "Ye shall be baptized with the Holy Ghost not many days hence;" and in chap. ii. 4 we are told, "They were all filled with the Holy Ghost." So far as I can understand, therefore, they are one and the same thing, and the writer of the Acts throughout prefers the word "filling." It recurs like the chime of a peal of bells, borne by the fitful breeze across the valley of the centuries. In any case let us see to it that we know what the filling is; it will be time enough then to discuss the baptism.

Say not that this filling by the Spirit was for the first Christians and not for us. Certainly His gifts were part of the special machinery needed to impress the Gentile world; but the filling of the Spirit is conterminous with no one age. Alas! that many think that the Almighty, like some bankrupt builder, constructed the portico of His Church with marble, and has finished it with common brick! What does the Apostle mean (Eph. v. 18) when he bids us "Be filled with the spirit?" We appropriate the doctrines the exhortations, the mystic teachings of that glorious epistle. Why then should we overlook this distinct command, which demands the obedience of all to whom the epistle comes? Let us never forget also that God's biddings are His enablings, and that what He commands the universal Church He is prepared to accomplish for each individual member of it.

Nothing could be clearer than the announcement of the Apostle Peter on the day of Pentecost, that the promise was not to themselves only, but *to all that are afar off, even as many as the Lord our God shall call* (Acts ii. 39). Have you been called, my reader to the grace of God? Then the promise of being filled is as much for you in the westering light of this age, as it was for those who lived in its silver dawn. Appropriate it.

We must appropriate the filling power of the Holy Spirit as we do all God's gifts by faith. Do not prepare yourself to receive it. Do not attempt a renovation of the inner life as the condition for His entrance, for your utmost preparations will be made in vain. Do not try to make room for Him. Simply be willing to yield your whole being to His grace, and believe that just as the earthly parent gives to the child all good and needful things as soon as the request is made, so will our Father in heaven give the filling of the Spirit to each child that asks for it. Ask for it in humble consciousness of your own unworthiness, but with eager desire that you may be the better able to glorify God. Wait in the surrender and stillness of your heart, like that which hushed the Tabernacle before the ark, where Samuel slept. And believe that there and then God does keep His word with your soul, and that "the Lord suddenly comes to His temple."

Then rise up and go forth from your chamber, not trying to feel filled, but reckoning that God has kept his word with you, and daring to believe it, though you may not be conscious of any emotional outburst. And you will find when you come to work or suffer or meet temptation, that there will be in you the consciousness of a power which you have never known before, and which will indicate the filling of the Holy Spirit.

But remember it is not enough to be filled once for all. Like the Apostles of old, we must seek perpetual refillings. They who were filled in the second chapter of Acts were filled again in the fourth. Happy is that man who never leaves his chamber in the morning without definitely seeking and receiving the plenitude of the Spirit! He shall be a proficient scholar in God's school, for the anointing which he has received, like fresh oil, shall abide in him, and teach him all things. Above all, he will be taught the secret of abiding fellowship with Christ, for it is written, "As it hath taught you, ye shall abide in Him" (1 John ii. 27).

It is all-important also to remember that just as a fire cannot be maintained without freshly heaped-up fuel, so the energetic working of the Holy Spirit in human hearts is largely dependent on the daily devout study of the Word of God. It is through the word that the Spirit effects the fullness of His work on those that receive Him.

There is nothing more to be said now. It is doubtless true that we may be filled with the Holy Spirit from our conversion; but since this is not the general experience of Christians, let us examine where we stand, and, if needs be, ask for that which might have been ours long years ago, if only we had sought it.

The Secret of Power

Do you not sometimes moan over your want of power? You stand face to face with devil-tormented people, but you cannot cast the devil out. You feel that you ought to confess Christ in the workshop, the commercial room, the railway carriage, and the home, but your lips refuse to utter the message of the heart. Yes, and worse than all, you are constantly being overcome by besetting sins, which carry you whither you would not. There is a lamentable lack of power amongst us. Not many can roll back the tide of battle from the gates, nor wield the weapons, which were child's play to the saints of olden times.

I learnt a lesson about this the other day in my Firewood Factory, where we provide employment for men and boys. We use a circular saw for cutting through the beams of solid timber. Until recently, this saw was worked by a crank, turned by twelve to fifteen men. But it was slow, hard, and expensive work. At last we were driven to something more expeditious and bought a gas-engine. And now the saw, driven by this engine, does in two or three hours as much work as it did formerly in a day, and at less than a tenth of the cost. It is the same saw, but the difference lies in the power that drives it. It used to be driven by hand-power, now it is driven by an equivalent for steam, and the only thing we need to do is to keep the connecting band tight.

It is not a question as to our abilities or qualifications, but of the power behind us. If that is nothing more than human, it is not surprising that the results are miserably poor. But if we link ourselves to the Eternal Power of God, nothing will be impossible to us. "All things are possible to him that believeth." The great matter is to see that the connecting band of Faith is in good use. Apart from the vine the branch can do nothing.

But where can I find the Power of God?

Jesus Christ is the reservoir in which the Power of God is stored. "It pleased the Father that in Him should all fullness dwell." All power is His. He would not receive it from the devil on the mountain of temptation, but He laid claim to it on the mountain of Ascension. Listen to His majestic words, "All power is given me in heaven and on earth." In that august moment He united in Himself the power, which He had as the Son of man, with the power He had with the Father before the world was. And now all power resides in Him forever more, not for Himself only, but for us.

How may I get this power for myself?

By faith. Each time you are face to face with some difficulty, or temptation, or service, lift up your heart to the living Saviour, draw upon Him, let Him feel that you are depending upon Him for the word to say, and the strength to say it. And immediately there will be a willing up of power within your heart, as lakes are filled from hidden springs.

But my faith is so weak, I forget to look in my hour of need; and when I do look it does not seem to give me much help.

Weak faith generally shows that there is something wrong in the inner life. Examine yourselves to see the cause. Are you yielding to temptation? Every temptation overcome is an increase of spiritual power, but every temptation yielded to cuts the sinews of your strength and shears off the seven locks of your might. Have you fully yielded yourself to God? Often failure points to lack of consecration. Is not self too prominent in you? Before conversion you lived from the center of an irreligious self. Are you perfectly sure that you are not now living from the center of a religious self?

Show me the workings of this religious self, the symptom and source of weakness, that I may know and hate myself.

Think for a moment! In making plans for doing God's work, do you not often act upon your own impulse, instead of waiting to inquire His will? Have you not often rushed into an enterprise without once considering whose spirit it was that prompted you? Do you not continually ask God to help you in all your little schemes, without first asking if He approved of them, or seeking to know what He had on hand, and if you might help Him? And when all is done, is there not a spirit of self-congratulation, which, though it array

42

itself in the garb of humility, is most distasteful to Him, who resisteth the proud?

How may I be different? I am prepared to forego anything, if only I may win this blessed secret of blessing, and saving others.

Then yield to Jesus your whole self. You are His by the purchase of His blood, now be His by your own glad choice. Bind yourself as a sacrifice to the horns of the altar. Present your body, soul, and spirit. Hand yourself over to be His. Ask Him to come and take you. Tell Him that, from this glad hour, you wish to be made willing to have His way. His will, His law in all. Go through life saying, a thousand times each day, I am His.

But if I try to give myself thus wholly to Him, how shall I know that He takes me?

At the first, you can only know it by faith. He pledges His word to take that which is given Him. If you give your self or try to give yourself, or will to give yourself, He instantly takes you to be His, and from that moment you are His in the bonds of an ownership, which is the daybreak of Love and Power and Blessing. At first there may be no gracious response of emotion, but, as the days pass on, and you come to taste more and more the sweetness of belonging, nevermore to yourself, but only to Him, there will come into your heart the fullness of joy, as well as the fullness of power. You may not be conscious of having much power, or any, before you begin to work, but when you have begun you will be aware that there is going forth from you a virtue which will make the commonest words powerful as that garment hem which brought healing to the trembling woman.

But how shall I remain in this blessed state?

Jesus will see to that. Trust Him to keep you trusting. At first it may be an effort to keep yourself in the love of God, but it will become easier, until at last it is a second nature. Then you will think more of what He says to you than of what you say to Him. Then you will be always on the alert to catch the least whisper of His voice, the slightest token of His will. Then you will bring every plan and purpose into the King's weigh-house before putting them in action, or even submitting them to your dearest friend. Then you will always feel that you are a member of His body, depending for the least direction, and for all needed strength on Him, the Head. Then there will be ever on your lips the words, "What next, dear Lord, what next?" and you shall read His will in circumstances, which to others might seem trivial and devoid of meaning. You will be always on the alert to find out for each day what good works have been prepared by Him for you to walk in. All that happens to you shall be as couriers bringing the secret letters of His love, signed by His hand, and telling you what to do. Nothing shall seem to come amiss or by chance. In all things you shall have definite fellowship with Him, until you talk over with Him all your life. You shall abide in Him, and He in you, and out of that abiding union will come abiding power, because His power shall reside in you in all its glory, just as the flashing volume of the cataract dwells constantly in the rocky basin into which it falls, and from which it rushes forth to ward drought and famine from the fields and homes of men.

It is a fair vision, and I would that my poor life might touch even its outermost rim of beauty, but I fear it is not for me.

Aye, but it is, if only you are content to open the door to Him. He stands at the door and knocks; if any will open the door He will come in. Are you willing to let Him in? Are you willing for Him to do what He likes with you and yours? Are you willing to be an ass's jaw-bone in the hands of this Samson, a cypher behind this mighty numeral? If so, He will begin to fulfill in you the good pleasure of His goodness and the work of faith with power; and you may write on the lintel of your life, "This house has passed into other hands, and will be opened under entirely new management." You cannot help being full of power if the Almighty Saviour comes to live in you. If you want overcoming power, get the Overcomer to come and fill you, and the thing is done. Do not talk about *it*, but about Him; it is not an influence, it is Himself.

This is my will, most merciful Lord, and from this moment grant that I may always desire and will that which is to Thee most acceptable and most dear. Let Thy will be mine, and let my will ever follow Thine, and agree perfectly with it, as the steel to the magnet, or the hand to the head.

But there is something in addition, which you must mark and remember. The reading of the Bible is as necessary as the fuelling of an engine with coal, or the imparting of strength to an invalid by food. And this reading must be steeped in the spirit of prayer. You must never let your work for Christ so engross you, as to rob you of those quiet hours, when He needs you to be alone with Him, that He may declare to you His Father's Name, and reveal Himself, and charge you with the spiritual forces stored up in Him. It will be well to keep yourself free from attractive avenues of service to be fresh for those still hours. They are more dear to Him, and more needful for you, than all your service. "In earing time and harvest thou shalt rest." One hour spent in work, after prolonged fellowship with Christ, will pay better than twelve hours spent in unbroken toils. Christ cares less for the amount of work done than for its quality. He is more anxious about the worker than the work.

Help me to remember this. Thou Lord of the harvest, and often may I leave even the whitening fields, that in Thee I may find rest and strength. And if I seem to tarry, I pray Thee, send some loving reminder to call me to Thy side, as Thou didst to Mary by the hand of her sister Martha.

Stay, one moment. There is one blessed secret more. When the Apostles were eager to win the world. He kept them waiting for ten long days, not that He was indifferent to the claims of a perishing race, nor to damp their ardor, but because they had not received that induement of Power, which is the prerogative of the Holy Ghost to impart. Perhaps you lack this. You have received Him as Comforter, Teacher, Sanctifier, but not yet as Power for Service. But He will be this ta you, if you will. "Be filled with the Spirit" is a positive command. All you have to do is to make room for Him, and this sacred wind will come in through every chink, and key-hole, and aperture, and you will unconsciously become filled with spiritual might; "strengthened with all might by His Spirit in your inner man."

And when the Power of the Highest overshadows our meek and waiting souls, who shall estimate the results that shall accrue to His glory? This is the dying need of the Church. This is the one condition of her success. But it can only be hers by prayer and fasting. If only she would never rest till she obtained it, watching daily at His gates, waiting at the posts of His doors, seeking it as silver, and searching for it as a hid treasure, then she would do exploits as of old, and look forth as the morning, "fair as the moon, clear as the sun, and terrible as an army with banners."

If you win this power, beware that you do not lose it. If a man sits on a chair, the feet of which stand on glass castors, you may pour a continual stream of electricity into him, and it will remain in him, not a spark will be lost, every part of his body will be charged with it. But if there is so much as a thread connecting his body with the earth, all the electric current will pass away, as water through the cracks of ajar. So will one besetting sin, one evil motive, one proud thought indulged in and permitted, rob us of the might of the Holy Ghost. Let us beware!

"And the Lord looked on him, and said. Go in this thy might; have not I sent thee?"

The Lost Chord Found

THE story of the lost chord has been told in exquisite verse, and in stately music. We have all heard of the lady, who in the autumn twilight, which softly filled the room, laid her fingers on the open keys of a glorious organ. She knew not what she was playing, or what she was dreaming then; but she struck one chord of music, like the sound of a great amen.

> It flooded the crimson twilight,
>   Like the close of an angel's psalm;
> And it lay on her fevered spirit
>   With a touch of infinite calm.
>
> It quieted pain and sorrow,
>   Like love overcoming strife;
> It seemed the harmonious echo
>   From our discordant life.
>
> It linked all perplexed meanings,
>   Into one perfect peace;
> And trembled away into silence
>   As if it were loth to cease.

Something called her away, and when she returned to the organ, she had lost that chord divine. Though she longed for it, and sought it, it was all in vain. It was a lost chord.

Whenever I hear that story, it reminds me of the lost joy, the lost peace, the lost power, of which so many complain. At the beginning of their Christian life, near at hand, or right back in the past, it would seem as if they had struck the chord of a blessed and glorious life. As long as those notes lingered in their lives, they were like the days of heaven upon earth, but alas! they died away soon into silence — and all their life is now filled with regret for the grace of days that are dead.

> Where is the blessedness I knew
>   When first I saw the Lord?
> Where is the soul-refreshing view
>   Of Jesus and His Word?
>
> What peaceful hours I then enjoyed!
>   How sweet their memory still!
> But they have left an aching void,
>   The world can never fill.

These words are written to help all such and to give them again the sweet lost chord. Take heart! you may again have all, and more than all that you have ever lost. You have flung your precious stones into the deep, there has been a moment's splash, a tiny ripple, and they have sunk down and down, apparently beyond hope of recovery. Yet the hand of Christ will again place them on your palm. Only henceforth, be wise enough to let Him keep them for you.

These are the steps back — steps you may take at once: —

1. — *Be sure that God will give you a hearty Welcome.* He is not an angry Judge. He has not given you up or ceased to love you. He longs after you. His portrait is drawn by One who could not mislead us, who compares Him to the Father of a loved and prodigal boy, ever watching from His windows the road by which the truant went, eagerly longing for his return, and ready, if he should see him a great way off, to run to meet him, and clasp him, rags and filth and all, to his yearning heart. That is thy God, my friend. Listen to His words, broken by sighs, "How shall I give thee up, Ephraim? how shall I deliver thee, Israel? how shall I make thee as Admah? how shall I set thee as Zeboim? Mine heart is turned within Me, My compassions are kindled." Read the last chapter of the Book of Hosea, which may be well called the backsliders' gospel. Read the third chapter of Jeremiah, and let the plaintive pleadings to return soak into your spirit. Read the story of Peter's fall and restoration, and let your tears fall thick and fast on John xxi., as you learn how delicately the Lord forgave, and how generously He intrusted the backslider with His sheep and lambs. Be sure that though your repeated failures and sins

46

have worn out everyone else, they have not exhausted the infinite love of God. He tells us to forgive our offending brother unto four hundred and ninety times, how much oftener will He not forgive us? According to the height of heaven above the earth, so great is His mercy. "Let the wicked forsake his way, and the unrighteous man his thoughts, and let him return unto the Lord, and He will have mercy upon him, and to our God, for He will abundantly pardon." If you go back to God, you are sure of a hearty welcome.

2. — *Seek to know and confess whatever has come between God and you.* You have lost the light of God's face, not because He has arbitrarily withdrawn it, but because your iniquities have come between you and your God, and your sins, like a cloud before the sun, have hid His face from you. Do not spend time by looking at them as a whole, deal with them one by one. The Boer is a formidable foe to the British soldier, because he is trained from boyhood to take a definite aim and bring down his mark, while our soldiers fire in volleys. In dealing with sin, we should imitate him in the definiteness and accuracy of his aim. Ask God to search you and show you what wicked way is in you. Marshal all your life before Him, as Joshua marshaled Israel, sift it through, tribe by tribe, family by family, household by household, man by man, until at last you find the Achan who has robbed you of the blessed smile of God. Do not say: Lord, I am a great sinner, I have done what I ought not, I have not done what I ought. But say. Lord, I have sinned in this, and this, and that, and the other. Call up each rebel sin, by its right name, to receive sentence of death. Your heart is choked with sins; empty it out, as you would empty a box, by handing out first the articles that lie on the surface. When you have removed them, you will see more underneath; hand them out also. When these are removed, you will probably see some more. Never rest till all are gone. Confession is just this process of telling God the unvarnished story — the sad, sad story — of each accursed sin. How it began. How you sinfully permitted it to grow. How you have loved and followed it to your bitter cost.

3. — *Believe in God's instant forgiveness.* How long does it take you to forgive your child, when you are sure that it is really sorry and repentant? Time is not considered in forgiveness. The estrangement of a lifetime, the wrongdoing of years may be forgiven in the twinkling of an eye, in the time that a tear takes to form and fall. So it is with God. If we confess our sins. He is faithful and just to forgive us. He does sometimes keep us waiting for an answer to other prayers, but He never keeps us waiting one single second for an answer to our prayer for forgiveness. It is hardly possible for the prodigal to stammer out the words: Father, I have sinned, before the answer flashes upon him, I have put away thy sin, thou shalt not die. There is not a moment's interval between the humble and sad telling of the story of sin and God's forgiveness. As soon as a penitent appears in the doorway of God's throne-room, the golden scepter of His royal forgiveness is stretched out for him to touch. You may not feel forgiven. You may have no ecstasy of joy. But you are forgiven, in the thoughts of God. The angels hear Him say: *Child, thy sins,*

which are many, are all forgiven thee; go in peace. If we confess, and as soon as we confess, He is faithful and just to forgive. He never says. Go thy way, and return to-morrow, and I will see whether I can forgive. He hates the sin, and is only too glad to sweep it away. He loves the sinner, and is only too happy to receive him again to His embrace. And He is able to do all this so quickly and so entirely, because Jesus Christ our Lord bare our sins in His own body on the tree.

4:.— *Give up the cause of past failure.* True repentance shows itself in eager care not to offend again. This care prompts the sinner to go back on his past life to discover how it was that he came to sin, and to avoid the cause. Is it a friendship? Then he will cut the tender cord, though it were the thread of his life. Is it an amusement? Then he will forever absent himself from that place, those scenes, and that companionship. Is it a profitable means of making money? Then he will rather live on a crust than follow it a moment longer. Is it a study, a pursuit, a book? Then he will rather lose hand, or foot, or eye, than miss the favor of God, which is life. Is it something that the Church permits? Nevertheless, to him it shall be sin. If you cannot walk on ice without slipping or falling, it is better to not go on at all. If you cannot digest certain food, it is better not to put it in the mouth. It may seem impossible to extricate yourself from certain entanglements which have woven themselves about you. Nevertheless, remember Him who said, Let My people go, that they may serve Me. He cut the knot for them; if you trust Him, He will cut it for you. Or if He do not cut it at a single blow. He will untie it by the patient workings of His Providence.

5. — *Take any public step that may be necessary.* It is not enough to confess to God; you must also confess to man, supposing that you have sinned against him. Leave your gift at the altar and go to be reconciled to thy brother. If you have done him a wrong, go and tell him so. If you have defrauded him, whether he knows or not, send him the amount you have taken or kept back, and add to it something to compensate him for his loss. Under the Levitical law it was enacted that the delinquent should restore that which he took violently away, or that about which he had dealt falsely, and should add one fifth part thereto, and only then might he come with his trespass offering to the priest, and be forgiven. This principle holds good to-day. You never will be happy till you have made restitution. Write the letter or make the call at once. And if the one whom you defrauded is no longer alive, then make the debt right with his heirs and representatives. You must roll away this stone from the grave, or the dead joy can never arise, however loudly you may call it to come forth. I do not believe in a repentance which is not noble enough to make amends for the past, so far as they may lie within its reach.

6. — *Give your whole heart once and forever to God.* You may have done it before, but do it again. You may never have done it, then do it for the first time. Kneel down and give yourself, your life, your interests, your all to God. Lay the sacrifice on the altar. If you cannot *give,* then ask God to come, and

take. Tell Him that you wish to be only, always, all for Him. We might well hesitate to give the Glorious Lord such a handful of withered leaves, if He had not expressly asked us each to give Him our heart. It is very wonderful; but He would not make such a request if He did not really mean it. No doubt He can make something out of our poor nature. A Vessel for His Use. A Weapon for His Hand. A Receptacle for His Glory. A Crown for His Brow.

7. — *Trust God to keep you in all the Future*. The old version used to tell us that He was able to keep us from falling. The new version, giving a closer rendering of the Greek, tells us that He is able to guard us from stumbling. So He can. So He will. But we must trust Him. Moment by moment we must look into His face, and say, "Hold Thou me up, and I shall be safe; keep me as the apple of Thine eye; hide me under the shadow of Thy wings." He will never fail thee. He will never fail thee nor forsake thee. He will give His angels charge to keep thee in all thy ways. He will cover thee with His feathers, and under His wing thou shalt trust.

But you say, I fail to look at the moment of temptation. Then do this. Ask the Holy Spirit, whose office it is to bring all things to our remembrance, that He would remind you to look off to Jesus, when you are in danger. Intrust yourself each morning into His hands. Look to Him to keep you looking. Trust in Him to keep you trusting. Do not look at your difficulties or weaknesses. Do not keep thinking that you will some day fall again. Go through life, whispering, saying, singing, a thousand times a day, *Jesus saves me now*.

A friend once told me, that she had been kept from backsliding thus: — She always took time at night to consider quietly in the presence of God, where she had lost ground during the day, and if she felt that she had done so, she never slept until she had asked to be forgiven and restored. 'Tis a good expedient, dear reader, for thee and me. Let us repair the little rift within the lute, lest by-and-by it spread and make our music mute, and slowly widening, silence all.

If these directions are followed, the lost chord will be no longer lost, nor shall we have to wait until God's great Angel sounds it, but it will ring again in our heart, and make sweet music in our life.

The Secret of Victory Over Sin

THE longer I live, and learn the experience of most Christian people, the more I long to help them and unfold glimpses of that Life of Peace, and Power, and Victory over sin, which our heavenly Father has made possible for us. There are blessed secrets in the Bible, hidden from the wise and prudent, but revealed to babes; things which eye hath not seen, or ear heard, or the heart of man conceived, but which God reveals by His Spirit to them that love Him; and if these were once understood and accepted, they would wipe away many a tear, and shed sunshine on many a darkened pathway.

49

The bitterest experience with most Believers is the Presence and Power of Sin. They long to walk through this grimy world with pure hearts and stainless garments. But when they would do good, evil is present with them. They consent to God's law that it is good; they approve it; they even delight in it after the inward man; they endeavor to keep it; but, notwithstanding all, they seem as helpless to perform it as a man, whose brain has been smitten with paralysis, to walk straight. What rivers of briny tears have fallen upon the open pages of the Penitents' Psalm (51st), shed by those who could repeat it every word from the heart! And what regiments of weary feet have trodden the Bridge of Sighs, if we may so call Romans vii., which sets forth, in vivid force, the experience of a man who has not learnt God's secret!

Surely our God must have provided for all this. It would not have been like Him to fill us with hatred to sin, and longings for holiness, if there were no escape from the tyranny of the one, and no possibility of attaining the other. It would be a small matter to save us from sinning on the other side of the pearly gate; we want to be saved from sinning now, and in this dark world. We want it for the sake of the World, that it may be attracted and convinced. We want it for our own peace, which cannot be perfected whilst we groan under a worse than Egyptian bondage. We want it for the Glory of God, which would be then reflected from us, with undimming brightness, as sunshine from burnished metal.

What then, does the Word of God lead us to expect? Before Abraham arose to walk through the land of Promise in its length and breadth, God bade Him "lift up his eyes and look." And before we can enter into the enjoyment of our privileges in Jesus Christ, we must know what they are, in something of their length and breadth, and depth and height.

1. — *We must not expect to be free from temptation.* Our adversary the devil is always going about as a roaring lion seeking whom he may devour. He tempted our Lord, he will tempt us. He will entice us to do wrong by every avenue of sense, and will pour his evil suggestions through eye and ear, and touch, and mouth, and mind. If he does not attack us himself, he can set on us any one of his myriad agents, who will get behind us, and step softly up to us, and whisperingly suggest many grievous blasphemies which we shall think have proceeded from our own mind.

But Temptation is not Sin. A man may ask me to share with him the spoils of a burglary, but no one can accuse me of receiving stolen property if I indignantly refuse and keep my doors close shut against him. Our Lord was tempted in all points as we are, yet without sin. You might go through hell itself, teeming with all manner of awful suggestions, and yet not sin. God would not allow Satan to tempt us, if temptation necessarily led to sin; but temptation does not do so; there is no sin, so long as the Will refuses to consent to the solicitation, or catch at the bait.

Temptation may even be a blessing to a man, when it reveals to him his weakness, and drives him to the Almighty Saviour. Do not be surprised, then, dear child of God, if you are tempted at every step of your earthly journey, and almost beyond endurance, but you will not be tempted beyond what you are able to bear, and with every temptation there will be a way of escape.

2. — *We must not expect to lose our sinful nature*. When we are born again, a new life, the life of God, is put into us by the Holy Spirit. But the old self-life, which is called in Scripture the flesh, is not taken away. The two may co-exist in the same heart. "The flesh lusteth against the Spirit, and the Spirit against the flesh." The presence of this old self-life within our heart may be detected by its risings, rufflings, chafings, and movings towards sin when temptation calls to it from without. It may be as still as death before the increasing power of the new life, but it will still be present in the depths of our nature, as a Samson in the dark dungeons of Philistia, and there will be always a possibility, and a fear, of its strength growing again to our shame and hurt.

Do not ignore the presence of a sinful nature within you, with its tendencies and possibilities for sin. Many souls have been betrayed into negligence and un watchfulness by the idea that the root of sin had been plucked from their hearts, and that therefore they could not sin again; and in the face of some sudden up-rising of their old nature they have been filled with agony and shame, even if they have not dropped for a moment back into a sea of ink. "If we say that we have no sin, we deceive ourselves, and the truth is not in us."

There is a difference between *sin* and *sins*. *Sin* is the root-principle of evil, the flesh, the old self-life, the bias and tendency to sin, which may be kept down by the grace of God, but which will remain in us, though in diminishing powder, till we leave this world. *Sins* are the outcome of this; the manifestations in act of the sinful nature within, from these we may be daily saved, through the grace of Jesus (Matt. i. 21). To put the matter clearly, *sin* is not dead in us, but we may be dead to *sin*, so that it shall not bear the deadly fruit of *sins*.

3. — *We must not expect to be free from liability to sin*. What is Sin? It is the "Yes" of the Will to temptation. It is very difficult to express the delicate workings of our hearts, but does not something like this happen to us when we are tempted? A temptation is suddenly presented to us, and makes a strong appeal. Immediately there may be a tremulous movement of the old nature, as the strings of a violin, or piano, vibrate in answer to any sounds that may be thrilling the air around. Some do not feel this tremulous response, others do, though I believe that it will get fainter and fainter as they treat it with continued neglect, so that at last, in the matured saint, it will become almost inaudible. This response indicates the presence of the evil nature within, which is in itself hateful in the sight of our Holy God, and should be bemoaned and confessed, and ever needs the presence of the Blood of Jesus to counteract and atone; but that tremulous movement has not, as yet, developed into an actual overt sin, for which we are responsible, and of which we need to repent.

Sin is the act of the Will, and is only possible when the will assents to some unholy influence. The Tempter, presenting his temptation through the senses and emotions, makes an appeal to the Will, which is our real self. If that Will instantly shudders, as chicks when the hawk is hovering in the sky above them, and cries, "How can I do this great wickedness, and sin against God!" and looks at once to Jesus, — there are, so far as I can understand, no sins. If on the other hand the Will begins to palter with temptation, to dally with it, and yield to it, then we have stepped out of the Light into the Dark, we have broken God's Law, splashed our white robes, and brought ourselves into condemnation. To this we are liable as long as we are in this world. We may live a godly, righteous, sober life for years, but if we look away from God, for only a moment, our will may be suddenly mastered, as was Louis XVIII. by the mob that invaded his palace, and we may, like David, be hurried into a sin, which will blast our peace and blacken our character for all coming time.

Now what are the secrets of victory over sin?

1. — *Remember that the blood of Jesus is ever at work cleansing you.* It is sweet to notice the present tenses of Scripture. He forgiveth, healeth, re-deemeth, crowneth, satisfieth, executeth judgment; but the sweetest of all is "The Blood of Jesus cleanseth from all sin." It cleansed us when first we knelt at His cross. It will cleanse away the last remnant of sin, as we cross the golden threshold. But it *does* cleanse us every hour; as the brook flows over the stones in its bed, till they glisten with lustrous beauty; and as the tear-water, pouring constantly over the eye, keeps it bright and clean, in spite of all the smuts that darken the air. The possession of a sinful nature is an evil that ever needs an antidote. The risings and stirrings of that nature beneath the appeals of temptation ever need cleansing. The permission of things in our life, which we now count harmless, but which we shall some day, amid increasing light, condemn and put away; — all these need forgiveness. But for all these needs there is ample provision for us in the Blood of Jesus, which is always crying to God for us. Even when we do not plead it. or remember it, or realize our need of it, it fulfills for us and in us its unceasing ministry of blessing.

2, — *Reckon yourself dead to the Appeals of Sin.* Sin has no power over a dead man. Dress it in its most bewitching guise, yet it stirs him not. Tears and smiles and words and blows alike fail to awaken a response from that cold corpse. No appeal will stir it now, until it hears the voice of the Son of God. This is our position in regard to the appeals of sin. God looks on us as having been crucified with Christ, and being dead with Him. In Him we have passed out of the world of sin and death into the world of resurrection glory. This is our position in the mind of God; it is for us to take it up, and make it real by faith. We may not feel any great difference, but we must believe that there is; we must act as if there were. Our children sometimes play at make-belief; we, too, are to make-believe, and we shall soon come to feel as we believe. When, then, a temptation solicits you, say, "I am dead to thee, spend not thine energies on one that is oblivious to thy spells and callous to thy charms, thou hast no more power over me than over my Lord and Head." "Reckon yourselves to be dead indeed unto sin, but alive unto God through Jesus Christ our Lord" (Rom. vi. 2).

3. — *Walk in the Spirit; keep in with the Holy Ghost.* The Holy Spirit is in the heart of every believer (Rom. viii. 9). But, alas, too often He is shut up in some mere attic in the back of the house, while the world fills the rest. And as long as it is so there is only one long, weary story of defeat and unrest. But He is not content. Know ye not that the Spirit, which He hath made to dwell in us, yearneth even unto jealous envy? (Jas. iv. 5, R. V.) Happy are they who yield to Him. Then He will fill them, as the tide fills the harbor and lifts the barges off" the banks of mud; He will dwell in them, shedding abroad the perfume of the Love of Jesus; and will reveal the deep things of God. We can always tell when we are wrong with the Spirit of God; our conscience darkens in a moment when we have grieved Him. And if we are aware of such a darkness, we do well never to rest until, beneath His electric light, we have discovered the cause, and confessed it, and put it away. Besides this, if we live and walk in the Spirit we shall find that He will work against the risings of our old nature, counteracting them as disinfecting powder counteracts the germs of disease floating in an infected house, *so that we may not do the things that we would* (Gal. v. 17, R. V.). This is one of the most precious words in the New Testament; if you have never tried it, I entreat you to begin to test it in daily experience. "Walk in the Spirit," hour by hour, by watchful obedience to His slightest promptings, and you will find that "you will not fulfill the lust of the flesh."

4. — *As soon as you are aware of Temptation, look instantly to Jesus.* Flee to Him quicker than a chick runs beneath the shelter of its mother's wing when the kestrel is in the air. In the morning, ere you leave your room, put yourself definitely into His hands, persuaded He is able to keep that which you commit unto Him. Go from your room with the assurance that He will cover you with His feathers, and under His wings shall you trust. And when the Tempter comes, look instantly up and say, "Jesus, I am trusting Thee to keep me." This is what the Apostle Paul calls using the shield of Faith. The upward glance of faith puts Jesus as a Shield between the Tempter and yourself. You may go through life, saying a hundred times a day, *Jesus saves me,* and He will never let those that trust in Him be ashamed. "He is able to guard you even from stumbling" (Jude 24, R. V.). You may be pressed with temptations from without, and may feel the workings of evil within, and yet your Will, looking earnestly to Jesus, shall remain steadfast, immovable, and unyielding, no weapon that is forged against you in the armory of hell shall prosper.

5. — *There is something better even than this.* It was first taught me by a grey-haired clergyman, in the study of the Deanery, at Southampton. Once, when tempted to, feel great irritation, he told us that he looked up and claimed the patience and gentleness of Christ; and since then it had become

the practice of his life to claim from Him the virtue, of which he felt the deficiency in himself. In hours of unrest, Thy Peace, Lord. In hours of irritation, Thy Patience, Lord. In hours of temptation. Thy Purity, Lord. In hours of weakness. Thy Strength, Lord. It was to me a message straight from the throne; till then I had been content with ridding myself of burdens; now I began to reach forth to positive blessing, making each temptation the occasion for a new acquisition of gold-leaf. Try it, dear reader.

When I have spoken thus, I have sometimes been met by the objection, "Ah, sir, it is quite true that the Lord will keep me if I look to Him, but I often forget to look in timey This arises from one of three causes. *Perhaps the heart and life have never been entirely surrendered to Jesus.* Constant defeat always indicates that there has been failure in consecration. You must not expect Christ to keep you, unless you have given your heart and life entirely over to Him, so that He is king. Christ cannot be keeper, if He is not king. And He will not be king at all, unless He is king in all. *Or perhaps there is a want of Watchfulness.* Christ will not keep us if we carelessly and wantonly put ourselves into the way of temptation. He will give His angels charge over us in every path of duty, but not to catch us every time we like to throw ourselves from the beetling height. Watch and pray that ye enter not into temptation. *Or perhaps there is a lack of feeding on the Word of God.* No one can live a life of Faith without seasons of prolonged waiting on God in the loving study of the Bible and in Prayer. The man who does not make time for private devotion in the early morning cannot walk with God all day. And of the two things, the devout meditation on the Word is more important to soul-health than even Prayer. It is more needful for you to hear God's words than that God should hear yours, though the one will always lead to the other. Attend to these conditions, and it will become both easy and natural to trust Christ in the hour of trial.

If, notwithstanding all these helps, you should be still betrayed into a sin, and overtaken by a fault, do not lose heart. If a sheep and a sow fall into a ditch, the sow wallows in it, the sheep bleats piteously until she is cleansed. Go at once to your compassionate Saviour; tell Him in the simplest words the story of your fall and sorrow; ask Him to wash you at once and restore your soul, and, whilst you are asking, believe that it is done. Then go to any one against or with whom you may have sinned and confess your faults one to another. Thus the Peace of God that passeth all understanding shall return to roost in your heart, and to guard it like a sentry-angel in shining armor.

And if you thus live, free from the power of sin, you will find that the Master will begin to use you as never before and to tell you His heart-secrets, and to open to you the royal magnificence of a life hidden with Himself in God.

How to Bear Sorrow

YOU are passing through a time of deep sorrow. The love on which you were trusting has suddenly failed you, and dried up like a brook in the desert — now a dwindling stream, then shallow pools, and at last drought. You are always listening for footsteps that do not come, waiting for a word that is not spoken, pining for a reply that tarries overdue.

Perhaps the savings of your life have suddenly disappeared; instead of helping others you must be helped, or you must leave the warm nest where you have been sheltered from life's storms to go alone into an unfriendly world; or you are suddenly called to assume the burden of some other life, taking no rest for yourself till you have steered it through dark and difficult seas into the haven. Your health, or sight, or nervous energy is failing; you carry in yourself the sentence of death; and the anguish of anticipating the future is almost unbearable. In other cases there is the sense of recent loss through death, like the gap in the forest-glade, where the woodsman has lately been felling trees.

At such times life seems almost insupportable. Will every day be as long as this? Will the slow-moving hours ever again quicken their pace? Will life ever array itself in another garb than the torn autumn remnants of past summer glory? Hath God forgotten to be gracious? Hath He in anger shut up His tender mercies? Is His mercy clean gone forever?

This road has been trodden by myriads. When you think of the desolating wars which have swept through every century and devastated every land; of the expeditions of the Nimrods, the Nebuchadnezzars, the Timours, the Napoleons of history; of the merciless slave-trade, which has never ceased to decimate Africa; and of all the tyranny, the oppression, the wrong which the defenceless have suffered at the hands of their fellows; of the unutterable sorrows of women and children, surely you must see that by far the larger number of our race have passed through the same bitter griefs as those which rend your heart. Jesus Christ Himself trod this difficult path, leaving traces of His blood on its flints; and apostles, prophets, confessors, and martyrs have passed by the same way. It is comforting to know that others have traversed the same dark valley, and that the great multitudes which stand before the Lamb, wearing palms of victory, came out of great tribulation. Where they were we are; and, by God's grace, where they are we shall be.

Do not talk about punishment. You may talk of chastisement or correction, for our Father deals with us as with sons; or you may speak of reaping the results of mistakes and sins dropped as seeds into life's furrows in former years; or you may have to bear the consequences of the sins and mistakes of others; but do not speak of punishment. Surely all the guilt and penalty of sin were laid on Jesus, and He put them away forever. His were the stripes, and the chastisement of our peace. If God punishes us for our sins, it would seem that the sufferings of Christ were incomplete; and if He once began to punish us, life would be too short for the infliction of all that we deserve. Besides, how could we explain the anomalies of life, and the heavy sufferings of the saints as compared with the gay life of the ungodly? Surely, if our sufferings were penal, there would be a reversal of these lots.

Sorrow is a refiner's crucible. It may be caused by the neglect or cruelty of another, by circumstances over which the sufferer has no control, or as the direct result of some dark hour in the long past; but inasmuch as God has permitted it to come, it must be accepted as His appointment, and considered as the furnace by which He is searching, testing, probing, and purifying the soul. Suffering searches us as fire does metals. We think we are fully for God, until we are exposed to the cleansing fire of pain; then we discover, as Job did, how much dross there is in us, and how little real patience, resignation, and faith. Nothing so detaches us from the things of this world, the life of sense, the birdlime of earthly affections. There is probably no other way by which the power of the self-life can be arrested, that the life of Jesus may be manifested in our mortal flesh.

But God always keeps the discipline of sorrow in His own hands. Our Lord said, "My Father is the husbandman." His hand holds the pruning-knife; His eye watches the crucible; His gentle touch is on the pulse while the operation is in progress. He will not allow even the devil to have his own way with us. As in the case of Job, so always. The moments are carefully allotted. The severity of the test is exactly determined by the reserves of grace and strength which are lying unrecognized within, but will be sought for and used beneath the severe pressure of pain. He holds the winds in His fist, and the waters in the hollow of His hand. He dare not risk the loss of that which has cost Him the blood of His Son. "God is faithful, who will not suffer you to be tried above that ye are able."

In sorrow the Comforter is near. "Very present in time of trouble." He sits by the crucible, as a refiner of silver, regulating the heat, marking every change, waiting patiently for the scum to float away, and His own face to be mirrored in clear, translucent metal. No earthly friend may tread the winepress with you, but the Saviour is there. His garments stained with the blood of the grapes of your sorrow. Dare to repeat it often, though you do not feel it, and though Satan insists that God has left you, "*Thou art with me.*" Mention His name again and again, "*Jesus,* Jesus. Thou art with me." So you will become conscious that He is there.

When friends come to console you they talk of time's healing touch, as though the best balm for sorrow were to forget, or in their well-meant kindness they suggest travel, diversion, amusement, and show their inability to appreciate the black night that hangs over your soul, so you turn from them, sick at heart, and prepared to say, as Job of his, "Miserable comforters are ye all"; but all the while Jesus is nearer than they are, understanding how they wear you, knowing each throb of pain, touched by fellow-feeling, silent in a

56

love too full to speak, waiting to comfort from hour to hour as a mother her weary, suffering babe.

Be sure to study the art of this Divine comfort, that you may be able to comfort them that are in any affliction with the comfort with which you yourself have been comforted of God (2 Cor. i. 4). There can be no doubt that some trials are permitted to come to us, as to our Lord, for no other reason than that by means of them we should become able to give sympathy and succor to others. And we should watch with all care each symptom of the pain, and each prescription of the Great Physician, since, in all probability, at some future time, we shall be called to minister to those passing through similar experiences. Thus we learn by the things that we suffer, and, being made perfect, become authors of priceless and eternal help to souls in agony.

Do not shut yourself up with your sorrow. A friend, in the first anguish of bereavement, wrote, saying that he must give up Christian ministries in which he had delighted; and I replied immediately, urging him not to do so, because there is no solace for heart-pain like ministry. The temptation of great suffering is towards isolation, withdrawal from the life of men, sitting alone, and keeping silence. Do not yield to it. Break through the icy chains of reserve, if they have already gathered. Arise, anoint your head, and wash your face; go forth to do your duty, with willing though chastened steps. Self-ishness, of every kind, in its activities or its introspection, is a hurtful thing, and shuts out the help and love of God. Sorrow is apt to be selfish. The soul, occupied with its own griefs, and refusing to be comforted, becomes present-ly a Dead Sea, full of brine and salt, over which birds do not fly, and beside which no green thing grows. And thus we miss the very lesson that God would teach us. His constant war is against the self-life, and every pain He inflicts is to lessen its hold on us. But we may thwart His purpose, and extract poison from His gifts, as men get opium and alcohol from innocent plants.

A Hindoo woman, the beautiful Eastern legend tells us, lost her only child. Wild with grief, she implored a prophet to give back her little one to her love. He looked at her for a long while tenderly, and said, "Go, my daughter, bring me a handful of rice from a house into which Death has never entered, and I will do as thou desirest." The woman at once began her search. She went from dwelling to dwelling, and had no difficulty in obtaining what the proph-et specified; but when they had granted it, she inquired, "Are you all here around the hearth — father, mother, children — none missing?" But the peo-ple invariably shook their heads with sighs and looks of sadness; for far and wide as she wandered, there was always some vacant seat by the hearth. And gradually, as she passed on, the narrator says, the waves of her grief subsid-ed before the spectacle of sorrow everywhere, and her heart, ceasing to be occupied with its own selfish pang, flowing out in strong yearnings of sympa-thy with the universal suffering, tears of anguish softened into tears of pity, passion melted away in compassion, she forgot herself in the general inter-est, and found redemption in redeeming.

Do not chide yourself for feeling strongly. Tears are natural. Jesus wept. A thunder-storm without rain is fraught with peril; the pattering raindrops cool the air, and relieve the overcharged atmosphere. The swollen brooks indicate that the snows are melting on the hills and spring is near. "Daughters of Jerusalem," said our Lord, "weep for yourselves and your children." To bear sorrow with dry eyes and stolid heart may befit a Stoic, but not a Christian. We have no need to rebuke fond nature crying for its mate, its lost joy, the touch of the vanished hand, the sound of the voice that is still, provided only that the will is resigned. This is the one consideration for those who suffer — *Is the will right?* If it isn't, God Himself cannot comfort. If it is, then the path will inevitably lead from the valley of the shadow of death to the banqueting table and the overflowing cup.

Many say: I cannot feel resigned. It is bad enough to have my grief to bear, but I have this added trouble, that I cannot *feel* resigned. My invariable reply is: you probably never can feel resignation, but you can *will* it. The Lord Jesus, in the Garden of Gethsemane, has shown us how to suffer. He chose His Father's will. Though Judas, prompted by Satan, was the instrument for mixing the cup and placing it to the Saviour's lips, He looked right beyond him to the Father, who permitted him to work his cruel way, and said: "The cup that My Father giveth Me to drink, shall I not drink it?" And He said repeatedly, "If this cup may not pass from Me, except I drink it. Thy will be done." He gave up His own way and will, saying, "I will Thy will, O My Father; Thy will, and not Mine, be done."

Let all sufferers who read these lines go apart and dare to say the same words: "Thy will, and not mine; Thy will be done in the earth of my life, as in the heaven of Thy purpose; I choose Thy will." Say this thoughtfully and deliberately, not because you can feel it, but because you will it; not because the way of the cross is pleasant, but because it must be right. Say it repeatedly, whenever the surge of pain sweeps through you, whenever the wound begins to bleed afresh: Not my will, but Thine be done. *Dare to say Yes to God.* "Even so, Father, for so it seemeth good in Thy sight."

And so you will be led to feel that all is right and well; and a great calm will settle down on your heart, a peace that passeth understanding, a sense of rest, which is not inconsistent with suffering, but walks in the midst of it as the three young men in the fiery furnace, to whom the burning coals must have been like the dewy grass of a forest glade. "The doctor told us my little child was dying. I felt like a stone. But *in a moment* I seemed to give up my hold on her. She appeared no longer mine, but God's.

Be sure to learn God's lessons. Each sorrow carries at its heart a germ of holy truth, which if you get and sow in the soil of your heart will bear harvests of fruit, as seed-corns from mummy-cases fruit in English soil. God has a meaning in each blow of His chisel, each incision of His knife. He knows the way that He takes. But His object is not always clear to us.

In suffering and sorrow God touches the minor chords, develops the passive virtues and opens to view the treasures of darkness, the constellations of promise, the rainbow of hope, the silver light of the covenant. What is character without sympathy, submission, patience, trust, and hope that grips the unseen as an anchor? But these graces are only possible through sorrow. Sorrow is a garden, the trees of which are laden with the peaceable fruits of righteousness; do not leave it without bringing them with you. Sorrow is a mine, the walls of which glisten with precious stones; be sure and do not retrace your steps into daylight without some specimens. Sorrow is a school. You are sent to sit on its hard benches and learn from its black-lettered pages lessons which will make you wise forever; do not trifle away your chance of graduating there. Miss Havergal used to talk of "turned lessons."

Count on the afterward. God will not always be causing grief. He traverses the dull brown acres with His plough, seaming the yielding earth, that He may be able to cast in the precious grain. Believe that in days of sorrow He is sowing light for the righteous, and gladness for the upright in heart. Look forward to the reaping. Anticipate the joy which is set before you, and shall flood your heart with minstrel notes when patience has had her perfect work.

You will live to recognize the wisdom of God's choice for you. You will one day see that the thing you wanted was only second best. You will be surprised to remember that you once nearly broke your heart and spilt the wine of your life, for what would never have satisfied you if you had caught it, as the child the butterfly or soap-bubble. You will meet again your beloved. You will have again your love. You will become possessed of a depth of character, a breadth of sympathy, a fund of patience, an ability to understand and help others, which, as you lay them at Christ's feet for Him to use, will make you glad that you were afflicted. You will see God's plan and purpose; you will reap His harvest; you will behold His face, and be satisfied. Each wound will have its pearl; each carcase will contain a swarm of bees; each foe, like Midian to Gideon, will yield its goodly spoil.

The way of the cross, rightly borne, is the only way to the everlasting light. The path that threads the Garden of Gethsemane, and climbs over the hill of Calvary, alone conducts to the visions of the Easter morning and the glories of the Ascension mount. If we will not drink of His cup, or be baptized with His baptism, or fill up that which is behind of His sufferings, we cannot expect to share in the joy of His espousals and the ecstasy of His triumph. But if these conditions are fulfilled, we shall not miss one note in the everlasting song, one element in the bliss that is possible to men.

Remember that somehow suffering rightly borne enriches and helps mankind. The death of Hallam was the birthday of Tennyson's *In Memoriam*. The cloud of insanity that brooded over Cowper gave us, *God moves in a mysterious way.* Milton's blunders taught him to sing of Holy Light, *offspring of heaven first-born*, Rist used to say, "The dear cross has pressed many songs out of me." And it is probable that none rightly suffer anywhere without contributing something to the alleviation of human grief, to the triumph of good over evil, of love over hate, and of light over darkness.

If you believed this, could you not bear to suffer? Is not the chief misery of all suffering its loneliness, and perhaps its apparent aimlessness? Then dare to believe that no man dieth to himself. Fall into the ground, bravely and cheerfully to die; if you refuse this, you will abide alone, but if you yield to it, you will bear fruit which will sweeten the lot and strengthen the life of others who will never know your name, or stop to thank you for your help.

Peace, Perfect Peace!

"PEACE, perfect peace!" What music I there is in these words! The very mention of them fills the heart with longings, which cry out for satisfaction, and will not be comforted. Sometimes, indeed, we may succeed in hushing them for a little, as a mother does a fretful child; but soon they wall break out again with bitter and insatiable desire. Our nature sighs for rest, as the ocean shell when placed to the ear, seems to sigh for the untroubled depths of its native home.

There is peace in those silent depths of space, blue for very distance, which bend with such gentle tenderness over our fevered, troubled lives. There is peace in the repose of the unruffled waters of the mountain lake, sheltered from the wands by the giant cliffs around. There is peace at the heart of the whirlwind, which sweeps across the desert waste in whirling fury. The peace of a woodland dell, of a highland glen, of a summer landscape, all touch us. And is there none for us, whose nature is so vast, so composite, so wonderful?

There is. As Jacob lay a-dying in his hieroglyphed chamber, not far from the Pyramids, his face shadowed by approaching death, but aglow with the light of the world to which he was going, he told how Shiloh, the Peaceful One, the Peace-giver,, should come to give peace to men. Weary generations passed by and still he came not, until at length there stood among men One, whose outward life was full of sorrow and toil; but whose sweet calm face mirrored the unbroken peace that reigned within His breast. He was the promised Peace-giver. He had peace in Himself; for He said, "My peace." He had the power of passing that peace on to others; for He said, "My peace I *give* unto you." Why should not each reader of these lines receive the peace which Jesus had Himself, and which He waits to give to every longing and recipient heart?

A poor woman timidly asked the gardener of a gentleman's hothouse, if he would sell her *just one bunch of grapes for her dying child*. He gruffly threatened to summon the police, unless she quickly left the place. But as she sadly turned away, she was recalled by a girlish voice, bidding her stay, asking her story, and insisting on her having as many bunches as she could carry with her. And when she offered her few half-pence in return, she was met by the sweet, laughing answer, "Nay, my poor woman, this is my father's hothouse; we don't sell grapes here, but we are very pleased to *give* them; take them and welcome, for your dying child." It is so that Jesus *gives* His peace to all weary tired ones. Why not to you?

His peace is *perfect* (Isa. xxvi. 3). Unbroken by storms. Uninvaded by the rabble rout of care. Unreached by the highest surges of sorrow. Unstained by the contaminating touch of sin. The very same peace that reigns in Heaven, where all is perfect and complete.

His peace is *as a river* (Isa. xlviii. 18). The dweller on its banks, in time of drought, is well supplied with water. It is flowing at early dawn, as he goes to his daily toil. It is there in the scorching noon. It is there when the stars shine, hushing him to sleep with the melody of its waves. When he was a child, he plucked the flowerets on its banks; and when his foot shall tread its banks nevermore, his children's children shall come to drink its streams. Think, too, how it broadens and deepens and fills up, in its onward journey, and from its source to the boundless, infinite sea. So may our peace be, abiding and growing with our years.

His peace is *great* (Isa. liv. 13). The mountains may depart and the hills be removed, yet shall it abide. Its music is louder than the tumult of the storm. Learn the lesson of the Lake of Galilee; that the peace which is in the heart of Jesus, and which He gives to His own, can quell the greatest hurricane that ever swept down the mountain ravine and spent itself on the writhing waters beneath. For when the Master arose and rebuked the wind and said unto the sea, "Peace, be still," the winds ceased and there was a great calm. "Great peace have they which love Thy law, and nothing shall offend them."

His peace is *compatible with much tribulation* (John xvi. 33). If we never find our path dipping down into the sunless valley, we may seriously question whether we have not missed our way to the Celestial City. The road to the Mount of Ascension invariably passes through the shadowed Garden of Gethsemane, and over the steep ascent of Calvary, and then down into the Garden of the Grave. "We must, through much tribulation, enter the Kingdom of God." But amidst it all, it is possible to be kept in unbroken peace, like that which possessed the heart of Jesus, enabling Him calmly to work a miracle of healing amid the tumult of His arrest.

His peace *passeth all understanding* (Phil. iv. 7). It cannot be put into words. It defies analysis. It must be felt to be understood. The thing most like it is the gladsomeness of a child in its father's home, where wealth and love and wise nurture combine to supply all its need; but even that falls short of the glorious reality. "Eye hath not seen, nor ear heard, neither have entered into the heart of man, the things which God hath prepared for them that love Him; but God hath revealed them unto us by His Spirit. We have the mind of Christ." And (bringing out the deep meaning of the Greek), we may say, that

61

this peace will *sentinel* our hearts and minds, going to and fro, like a sentry before a palace, to keep off the intruders that would break in upon the sacred enclosure. Oh that we might be ever protected by a guardianship, so benign and watchful and invulnerable to attack.

There are a few conditions, however, which demand our careful thought.

1. — The Basis of Peace is the Blood. "He made peace by the Blood of His Cross" (Col. i. 20). We sometimes hear men speak of *making their peace with God*. But that is wholly needless. Peace has been made. When Jesus died on the Cross, He did all that needed to be done, and all that could be done, so far as God was concerned, in order to bring peace to men. Nothing more is requisite, save to lay aside fear and suspicion, and to accept the peace which He now sweetly and freely offers. "God was in Christ, reconciling the world unto Himself, not imputing their trespasses unto them...now be ye reconciled" (2 Cor. v. 19-20).

There were many obstacles to our peace, but they have been entirely met, and put out of the way. God's Holy Justice, which would pursue us with its drawn sword, can say nothing against us, because it has been more vindicated in the death of the Son of God, than it could have been in the perdition of myriads of worlds. The broken law, which might press its claims, is silenced by the full and complete satisfaction rendered it in the obedience and death of the Law-giver Himself. Conscience even, with its long and bitter record of repeated sin, feels able to appropriate forgiveness without scruple or alarm; because it understands that God can be just, and yet justify the believer in Jesus. "Who is he that condemneth? It is Christ that died; yea, rather that is risen again; who is even at the right hand of God; who also maketh intercession for us."

On the evening of His resurrection, our Lord entered through the unopened doors into the chamber where His disciples were cowering for fear of the Jews. His benediction, *Peace be unto you*, fell on their ears like the chime of bells amid the storm of Friburg's organ. But He did not rest satisfied with this. Indeed, His words alone would have been in vain. But when He had so said. He showed unto them His hands and His side, fresh from the Cross, with the marks of spear and nails, so that He stood amid them like a lamb, "as it had been slain." Do you wonder that they were glad? The heart must always be glad when it learns the sure basis of Peace in the Blood shed on the Cross. Best on that precious Blood; make much of it; remember that God sees it, even if you do not; be sure that it pleads through the ages, with undiminished efficacy; and be at peace.

2. — The Method of Peace is by Faith in God's Word. How many Christians miss God's peace because they look into their hearts to see how they feel. If they feel right and happy they are at peace. But if mists veil the inner sky, or the body is out of health, or the temperature of the heart is low, they become sad and depressed, and ill at ease. Peace has taken its flight. This will never do. Life is one long torture thus. This is not the blessed life which Jesus came to give us. To live like this is indeed to miss the prize of our high calling and to cast discredit on His dear Name. *If you seek peace through the medium of feeling you will seek it in vain.* It may come as a wayfaring man for a night, but it will not tarry. It may visit you like a transient gleam over the hillside, but it will be only a tiny break between long leagues of cloud. There is a more excellent way. Take up the Bible, the Word of God to *you.* Turn to some of the texts, which shine in its firmament, as stars of the first magnitude in the midnight sky. Consider, for instance words like these. Ponder them well. Seek not for frames, or feelings, or even for faith, but concentrate your mind and heart upon their mighty meaning.

"Whosoever *believeth* in Him, shall not perish, but have everlasting life" (John iii. 16).

"He that *heareth* My word, and believeth on Him that sent Me, hath everlasting life, and shall not come into condemnation, but is passed from death unto life" (John v. 24).

"By Him, *all that believe* are justified from, all things" (Acts xiii. 39).

"The blood of Jesus Christ cleanseth from *all* sin" (1 John i. 7).

What do these words mean? Can they mean one straw less than they say? And if they are as they seem, is it not clear, that directly you *believe,* you stand before God as a reconciled, accepted, and beloved child?

What is it to believe? It is to look up to Jesus, as a personal Saviour, handing over to Him the whole burden of your soul, for time and eternity; sure that He takes what you give, at the moment of your giving it, even though you feel no immediate peace or joy. Belief in the outset is trust.

"Your faith is so weak," But that does not matter, because there is not a word said about the amount of faith. The greatest faith could not make you more secure. The smallest faith cannot put you outside the circle of blessing; because the word, *believeth,* is so delightfully vague. Faith as a grain of mustard seed can move a mountain equally with faith as a walnut-shell. Faith that can only touch the garment hem gets a blessing which those who press may lose.

"You are not sure if you have the right faith." But all faith, any faith, is the right faith. There are not many sorts of faith. The faith that can only lay down its weary weight on Jesus; the faith that *tries* to look to Him; the faith that staggers towards Him and drops into His arms; the faith that cannot cling because its hands are so weak, but which calls to Him, believing that He can save, — That is all the faith you need, and having it you are saved.

"But you do not feel saved." And who said that that was an essential condition of salvation? Remember that it is one thing to be saved, and quite another to feel it. The one may exist without the other; and there are no doubt very many, who are certainly the children of God, but who have never had the sweet assurance of salvation, which is the seal of the Spirit, the blossom of grace, the kiss of God. *Directly you look to Jesus, you are saved, whether you*

feel it or not. Don't think about your feelings; don't think about your faith; look to Jesus; and reckon that God will keep His word, and save you.

The result of all this must inevitably be peace. Let Satan from without join with the timid heart within in threatening disaster; faith simply turns to the Word of God, and putting its finger on one of His exceeding great and precious promises, replies, "This must fail, ere I can perish; but I know whom I have believed, and am persuaded He will keep His word, and that He is able to keep that which I have committed unto Him."

3. — The Secret of Peace is the Constant Reference of all to the Care of God. "Be anxious in nothing; but in everything by prayer and supplication with thanksgiving let your requests be made known unto God; and the peace of God shall guard your hearts and your thoughts in Christ Jesus" (Phil. iv. 6-7). Acid dropped on steel, and allowed to remain there, will soon corrode it. And if we allow worries, anxieties, careworn questioning to brood in our hearts, they will soon break up our peace, as swarms of tiny gnats will make a paradise uninhabitable.

There is only one thing that we can do. We must hand them over to Jesus just as they occur. It will not do to wait until the day is done, but in the midst of its busy rush, whenever we are conscious of having lost our peace, we should stand still and ask the cause, and then lift up our hearts, and pass it off into the care of our loving and compassionate Lord. "'Tis enough that He should care, why should we the burden bear?"

Ah, what would not our days become, if only we could acquire this blessed habit? We look so weighted, and lead such burdened lives, because we do not trust Jesus with all the little worries of daily life. There is nothing small to Him if it hinders our peace. And when once you have handed aught to him, refuse to take it back again, and treat the tendency to do so as a temptation to which you dare not give way, no, not for a moment.

Care comes from many sources. Our daily food, our dear ones, our worldly prospects, our Christian work, our pathway in life, our growth in the Divine Life — all these contribute their quota to the total sum. Let us take them all, and lay them down at Jesus' feet, and leave them there; and then live looking to Him to do in us, with us, through us, for us, just as He will. And as we give Him our cares, He will give us His peace, and as He does so He will whisper, "My peace I give unto you, let not your heart be troubled, neither let it be afraid."

There is a remarkable text in Isaiah, which teaches us that the Government should be upon the shoulders of Jesus Christ; and that when it is so, there is no end to the increase of Peace. "*Of the increase of His government and peace there shall be no end* (ix. 7). Surely these glorious words refer, not only to the government of a nation, but of each individual life also, and they are very searching.

Where is the government of our lives? Is it in our own hands? Then we must not be surprised, if our hearts are like the troubled sea, when it cannot rest. We are out of harmony with God, and with His will, which must be done whether in us or in spite of us. There can be no Peace, because there is perpetual clashing, and rebellion.

But directly we put the government of our lives, down to their smallest details, into the hands of the Lord Jesus; then we enter into His own infinite Peace. And as His government is extended over our hearts and lives, so does our Peace extend, as when the blessed light of dawn spreads like a benediction through the world.

"In Me ye shall have peace." 'Twas our Saviour who said those words. Let us abide in Him. Let us live in Him. Let us walk in Him. Let us make of Him the secret place unto which we may continually resort. And as we are joined to Him, in the intimacy of deepest union, the peace that fills His heart, like a Pacific ocean, shall begin to flow into ours, until they are filled with the very fullness of God; and the peace of God, like a dove, with fluttering wings, shall settle down upon our hearts, and make them its home forevermore.

Seven Rules for Daily Living

THESE brief and simple words are intended for many earnest Christians who are dissatisfied with their present life, and long to enter that more blessed state of rest and peace of which they catch occasional glimpses; as white-plumaged sea-birds flash for a moment, faraway over the breakers, and then are lost to sight.

The visit of Messrs. Stanley Smith and Studd to Melbourne Hall will always mark an epoch in my own life. Before then my Christian life had been spasmodic and fitful; now flaming up with enthusiasm, and then pacing wearily over leagues of grey ashes and cold cinders. I saw that these young men had something which I had not, but which was within them a constant source of rest and strength and joy. And never shall I forget a scene at 7 a. m., in the grey November morning, as daylight was flickering into the bedroom, paling the guttered candles, which from a very early hour had been lighting up the page of Scripture, and revealing the figures of the devoted Bible-students, who wore the old cricketing or boating costume of earlier days, to render them less sensible of the raw, damp climate. The talk we held then was one of the formative influences of my life. Why should I not do what they had done? Why should I not yield my whole nature to God, working out day by day *that* which He would will and work within? Why should not I be a vessel, though only of earthenware, meet for the Master's use, because purged and sanctified?

There was nothing new in what they told me. They said, that "A man must not only believe in Christ for final salvation, but must trust him for victory over every sin, and for deliverance from every care." They said, that "The Lord Jesus was willing to abide in the heart which was wholly yielded up to Him." They said, that "If there were something in our lives that made it difficult for us to surrender our whole nature to Christ, yet if we were willing to be made willing to surrender them. He would make us not only willing, but glad." They said, that "Directly we give or attempt to give ourselves to Him, He takes us." All this was simple enough. I could have said it myself. But they urged me to take the definite step; and I shall be forever thankful that they did. And if in a distant country they should read this page, let them be encouraged to learn that one heart at least has been touched with a new fire, and that one voice is raised in prayer for their increase in the knowledge and love of Him who has become more real to the suppliant because of their brotherly words.

Very memorable was the night when I came to close quarters with God. The Angel that wrestled with Jacob had found me, eager to make me a Prince. There were things in my heart and life which I felt were questionable, if not worse; I knew that God had a controversy with respect to them; I saw that my very dislike to probe or touch them was a clear indication that there was mischief lurking beneath. It is the diseased joint that shrinks from the touch, the tender eye that shudders at the light. At the same time I did not feel willing to give these things up. It was a long struggle. At last I said feebly, "Lord, I am willing to be made willing; I am desirous that Thy will should be done in me and through me, as thoroughly as it is done in Heaven; come and take me and break me and make me." That was the hour of crisis, and when it had passed I felt able at once to add, "And now I give myself to Thee: body, soul, and spirit; in sorrow or in joy; in the dark or in the light; in life or in death, to be Thine only, wholly, and forever. Make the most of me that can be made for Thy glory." No rapture or rush of joy came to assure me that the gift was accepted. I left the place with almost a heavy heart. I simply assured myself that He must have taken that which I had given, and at the moment of my giving it. And to that belief I clung in all the days that followed, constantly repeating to myself the words, "I am His." And thus at last the joy and rest entered, and victory, and freedom from burdening care, and I found that He was moulding my will and making it easy to do what I had thought impossible; and I felt that He was leading me into the paths of righteousness for His name's sake, but so gently as to be almost imperceptible to my weak sight.

Now out of my own experience I would suggest these Seven Rules to my fellow-Christians:

1. — *Make a Definite Consecration of Yourselves to God.* Dr. Doddridge has left in his diary a very beautiful form of self-consecration. But you need not wait for anything so elaborate or minute as that. With most it would be sufficient to write out Miss Havergal's hymn, "Take my life and let it be," etc., and to sign their names at the foot. But in any case it is well to write down some record of the act, to keep for future reference. Of course when we have really given ourselves once, we cannot give ourselves a second time. We may renew the consecration vows, we may review the deed of gift, we may insert any new clauses we like. And if we have gone astray, we may ask the Lord to

forgive the foul wrong and robbery which we have done Him, and to restore our souls into the position from which we have fallen. Oh, how sweet the promise, "He restoreth my soul!" Dear Christian reader, seek some quiet spot, some still hour, and yield yourself to God.

2. — *Tell God that you are Willing to he made Willing about All.* A lady was once in great difficulties about certain things which she felt eager to keep under her own control. Her friend, wishful to press her into the better life of consecration, placed before her a blank sheet of paper, and pressed her to write her name at the foot, and then to lay it before God in prayer. She did so, and at once entered this blessed life. Are you willing to do this? Are you prepared to sign your name to a blank sheet of paper and then hand it over to God, for Him to fill in as He please? If not, ask Him to make you willing and able to do this and all things else. You never will be happy until you let the Lord Jesus keep the house of your nature, closely scrutinizing every visitor and admitting only His friends. He must reign. He must have all or none. He must have the key of every closet, of every cupboard, and of every room. Do not try to make them fit for Him. Simply give Him the key. And He will cleanse and renovate and make beautiful.

3. — *Reckon on Christ to do His Part Perfectly.* Directly you give, He takes. Directly you will open the door, He enters. Directly you will roll back the floodgates, He pours in a glorious tide of fullness: fullness of wealth, of power, of joy. The clay has only to be plastic to the hand of a Palissy. The marble has only to be pliant to the chisel of a Michael Angelo. The organ has only to be responsive to the slightest touch of a Handel. The student has only to follow the least hint of a Faraday or a Whewell. And there will be no failure, in results. Oh, to be equally susceptible to the moulding influences of Christ! "We shall not fail in realizing the highest ideal of which we are capable, if only we will let Him do His work unhindered.

4. — *Confess Sin Instantly.* If you allow acid to drop and remain on your steel fenders, it will corrode them, and if you will allow sin to remain on your hearts unconfessed, it will eat out all peace and rest. Do not wait for the evening to come, or until you can get alone, but *there* in the midst of the crowd, in the very rush of life, with the footprints of sin still fresh, lift up your heart to your merciful and ever-present Saviour, and say, "Lord Jesus, wash me now from that sin, in Thy precious blood, and I shall be whiter than snow." The blood of Jesus is ever at work, cleansing us from unconscious sin; but it is our part to apply for it to cleanse from conscious and known sins so soon as we are aware of their presence in our lives.

5. — *Hand over to Christ every Temptation and Care.* When you feel temptation approaching you, as a bird, by some quick instinct, is aware that the hawk is hovering near, then instantly lift your heart to Christ for deliverance. He cannot rebuff or fail you. "He will gather you under His feathers, and under His wings shall you trust." And when any petty annoyance or heavier worry threatens to mar your peace, in the flash of a moment, hand it over to

Jesus, saying, "Lord, I am oppressed, undertake this for me." Ah! you sigh, I wish indeed I could live like this, but in the moment of need I forget to look. Then do this. Trust in Christ to keep your trusting. Look to Him so to abide in you as to keep your abiding. In the early morning intrust to Him the keeping of your soul, and then as hour succeeds to hour expect Him to keep that which you have committed unto Him.

6. — *Keep in touch with Christ.* Avoid the spirit of fault-finding, criticism, uncharitableness, and anything inconsistent with His perfect love. Go where He is most likely to be found, either where two or three of His children are gathered, or where the lost sheep is straying. Ask Him to wake you morning by morning for communion and Bible-study. Make other times in the day, especially in the still hour of evening twilight, between the work of the day and the avocations of the evening, when you shall get alone with Him, telling Him all things, and reviewing the past under the gentle light which streams from His eyes.

7. — *Expect the Holy Ghost to work in, with, and for you.* When a man is right with God, God will freely use him. There will rise up within him impulses, inspirations, strong strivings, strange resolves. These must be tested by Scripture and prayer, and if evidently of God they must be obeyed. But there is this perennial source of comfort. God's commands are enablings. He will never give us a work to do without showing exactly how and when to do it, and giving us the precise strength and wisdom we need. Do not dread to enter this life, because you fear that God will ask you to do something you cannot do. He will never do that. If He lays aught on your heart, He will do so irresistibly; and as you pray about it the impression will continue to grow, so that presently, as you look up to know what He wills you to say or do, the way will suddenly open, and you will probably have said the word, or done the deed, almost unconsciously. Rely on the Holy Ghost to go before you, to make the crooked places straight, and the rough places smooth. Do not bring the legal spirit of "must" into God's free service. "Consider the lilies of the field, how they *grow.*" Let your life be as effortless as theirs, because your faith shall constantly hand over all difficulties and responsibilities to your ever-present Lord. There is no effort to the branch in putting forth the swelling clusters of grapes — the effort would be to keep them back.

There may be failures in this life, but they will arise on the human side, not the Divine. Well will it be if we can instantly discover the cause of failure, and confess it, and seek restoration to the old peace and joy. After all, the sheep does not keep the shepherd. The shepherd keeps the sheep, and feeds it, and leads it, and makes it to lie down. What then may we not expect from our Good Shepherd; and who can paint the verdure of the green pastures, or the crystal beauty of those unfailing springs, to which He will lead the docile and trustful spirit!

Be that spirit thine.

Seven Reasons for Believer's Baptism

THE longer I live, the more impressed I am with the beauty and significance of Believer's Baptism, and I cannot but feel, that if it were really thoroughly understood by Christian people, they would not hesitate to obey the Lord's command. Indeed, they would be eager to pass through the simple outward rite, which would express their desire to be as like Him as they may.

But remember at the outset that you may be baptized, as a believer, without becoming a member of the Baptist denomination. You may be baptized, and still continue in communion with that Christian body with which you have been accustomed to worship. This rite is a personal matter between the Lord and the individual believer.

Now Believer's Baptism differs from the ceremony which is often called Baptism, in two ways — First, in the Person baptized; and Second, in the mode of Baptism.

First, as to the Person Baptized. It must be *a believer,* one who believes in the Lord Jesus Christ. We sometimes hear people speak of *Adult* Baptism, but the expression is very misleading. If a man be as old as Methuselah, yet if he do not believe, he has no right to be baptized; whilst if a little child truly trust in the Saviour, it has an undeniable right to baptism. Christ did not ask for intense feeling or matured character, or years of consistency, as the condition of baptism. He only asked *faith*, "He that *believeth* and is baptized."... (Mark xvi. 16). The question in the baptism of the Eunuch (even though it be an interpolation) shows that it was the custom of the early Church to be sure of the *faith* of those who wished to be baptized (Acts viii. 37). And there is certain evidence that those baptized by the Apostles were true believers in the Lord. (*See references at the end.*) The only sort of baptism mentioned in the Bible is the Baptism of Believers; the sprinkling of babes, who cannot believe, may be a beautiful and interesting rite, but it does not fulfill the conditions of Believer's Baptism.

Second, as to the Mode of Baptism. It must be by immersion, *i.e.*, the dipping of the whole body beneath the water. If there were no other argument to prove that this was the ancient and scriptural mode, the question would be settled by an appeal to the *sixth chapter of the Ep. to the Romans.* The whole point of the argument there is this: the waters of Baptism are a Grave; Baptism is a Burial; the Baptized one is buried into the likeness of Christ's death.

If a few drops of water are sprinkled on the face, it is impossible to trace any resemblance to that eventful moment when Joseph and Nicodemus bore the lifeless body of the Lord to burial in the garden tomb, amid the tears of the Maries, and the evening fragrance of the spring flowers, and hid it from the sight of man. And what likeness is there to the resurrection of Christ, unless the whole body can be lifted from the grave-like waters into the upper air and light?

It is for these reasons, no doubt, that the prayer book of the Church of England in its rubric prescribes *immersion* as its usual mode of Baptism. No wonder that John baptized in Aenon "because there was much water there" (John iii. 23). And it was well that there was so ample a supply of water in Jerusalem, for the use of the priests and for temple purposes, otherwise the three thousand new-made converts could not have been baptized in one day (Acts ii. 41). It was in keeping with all this, that so many of the ancient churches were furnished with Baptistries. Of course, Baptism does not save. It has no sacramental efficacy. If a man is not saved before he is baptized, he certainly will not be saved by passing through that rite. In fact the ordinance will do him more harm than good.

Yet Believer's Baptism is binding on Christians for the following reasons:

1. — *Believers, should he Baptized, because the Lord Jesus was Baptized.* When He was thirty, He mixed with the crowds that thronged the banks of the Jordan, and asked baptism at the hands of John the Baptist. He that baptizes with fire was baptized with water (Matt. iii. 13; John i. 33). If there were no other reason for Believer's Baptism, would not this be enough? His footprints lead down into the deep clear waters, and if we would follow the Lamb wheresoever He goeth, we have no alternative than to follow Him there. It is enough for the servant to be as his Lord. He has left us an example that we should follow His steps. Courtiers will imitate the deformities of their King; let us imitate Christ in His fulfillment of all righteousness.

2. — *Believers should be Baptized; Christ commanded it.* "Go ye," said He, "and teach all nations, baptizing them" (Matt, xxviii. 19). These, as the Iron Duke once said, are the marching orders of the Church. We are not at liberty to alter or discuss them, we must simply obey. When a Roman Centurion said to his servant, *do this,* it was done immediately; and surely the Captain of our salvation should not be worse served by His disciples and friends. His mother spoke a memorable word to the Church of all time, when she said to the servants at Cana, "Whatsoever He saith unto you, do it." If we could see no meaning in this ordinance, we should submit to it, because He commanded it; how much more should we do so, when we can see its beauty and use. And all the time there rings in our hearing, like a peal of silver bells, these words, "If ye love Me, keep My commandments;" and may we not add, "His commandments are not grievous?" It is not enough to talk of love, let us show it.

3. — *Believers should be Baptized; the Apostles practiced it.* Wherever they went they employed the rivers and reservoirs for this holy rite. In Jerusalem (Acts ii. 41); in Samaria (viii. 12); in the Desert (viii. 36); amongst the Gentiles; in the house of the soldier Cornelius: and in the prison of the jailer at Philippi (Acts x. 48 and xvi. 33). Even if we had nothing else to go by, yet the practice of such men, who had so many opportunities of knowing the will of Christ, would be a conclusive guide of our duty. We refuse to stay with the corrupt Church of the fourth or fifth century; we will press back to the first,

70

when she had come fresh from the hand of her Lord. Her early practice shall be our guide.

4. — Bel*ievers should he Baptized; it is a beautiful symbol of the forgiveness of sin.* John the Baptist first used it for this object. "They were baptized of him in Jordan, *confessing their sins*" (Matt. iii. 6). Other meanings have gathered about the ordinance in addition to this, but this original one remains. Sin is constantly described as a moral *stain;* forgiveness is as constantly spoken of as *washing white* — whiter than the wreaths of driven snow. In Baptism, of course, all dust and impurity is removed from the body; and this outward cleansing is a sign and reminder of that which has already taken place in the Believer's Inner Experience. He seems to say, "I have alt ready plunged my sin-stained nature into the fountain opened for sin and uncleanness; nay, to make assurance doubly sure. I do now by faith repeat it; as my body is plunged into this crystal bath, so do I now plunge my whole being into the precious blood of Christ; and as my flesh is made perfectly clean by the water, so also is my spirit made clean by the application of the blood of Jesus Christ, God's Son, which cleanseth us from all sin" (1 John i. 7).

5. — *Believers should he Baptized; it is a Badge of Discipleship.* This is the meaning especially attached to it by Christ Himself. "Go ye, and *make disciples* of all nations, baptizing them." The Lord looked round for some world-wide substance, some universal act, which should serve as a badge of His disciples, and there was nothing so suitable as this. Water is everywhere, and few acts are more simple or common than the immersion of the bath. Alas! that it has become too much the badge of a sect. But let us not let Christ's idea be obscured by man's mistake. Believer's Baptism does not necessarily mean that you belong to the Baptist denomination. It means only that you are a disciple of Jesus Christ. There is no necessity, if you are baptized, that you should join the Baptists; you may be baptized as a disciple of the Saviour, and remain beneath any Church government you please. The Eunuch was baptized, but did not join a Church.

6. — *Believers should be Baptized; it marks a Break with the Old and a start for a New and Better Life.* Christ's Burial broke His Earthly Life into two parts. He was different on this side of the grave to what He was on the other. Physical weakness was replaced by Resurrection-life; dishonor by glory; weakness by power; a natural body by a spiritual body (1 Cor. xv. 43).

Something like this happens when a man trusts Christ. He dies and is buried to his old sinful past. He rises in the strength of Christ, into a new and glorious life. Now it is well to have an outward sign to impress all this on the Believer and on the World. And the Holy Ghost led the Apostles to put this new meaning into Baptism. "Know ye not, that so many of us as were baptized into Jesus Christ, were baptized into His death? Therefore we are buried with Him by baptism unto death; that like as Christ was raised up from the dead by the glory of the Father, even so we also should walk in newness of life" (Rom. vi. 4). When the Lord Jesus died, and was buried, all those who

71

in the thought of God are forever one with Him died with Him, and lay with Him in the grave, rising with Him in the light of the resurrection morning. And we have to appropriate these facts, and make them real by a living faith. Nor are they to be merely matters of sacred inner experience. As we set forth His death in the Lord's Supper, so we should set forth our death, in and with Him, in the Act of Baptism; whereby we are visibly buried in the likeness of His death, and raised in the likeness of His resurrection. It is a confession of our desire to be dead indeed to the world and to sin, and alive unto God, through Jesus Christ the Lord (Col. ii. 12, and iii. 1).

7. — *Believers should be Baptized; it is the Profession of a Creed*. When we are baptized, we profess to the world our belief of these distinct facts: — That Christ lived once upon our world in human flesh; that He died for our sins according to the Scriptures, and that He was buried; and that He rose again the third day according to the Scriptures; that He is living still; and that His word is law. The ordinance of baptism is a standing witness to the reality of those facts with which it is associated; and we should do all in our power to maintain and accentuate that evidence in the face of an unbelieving world.

For all these reasons, Believers should be Baptized. If you were baptized as a babe, you should be baptized again as a Believer (Acts xix. 3-5). Of course, as we cannot be saved by baptism, so we may be saved without it. The dying thief was never baptized, yet we know that he is in Paradise (Luke xxiii. 43). Thousands stand before the throne, clad in white raiment, who never passed through the waters of Baptism. But at the same time those who love are not always asking *what must I do*, but *what may I do*. We know that our salvation has been finished for us on the Cross, and it can make no difference to our final salvation whether we have been dipped or sprinkled. But it will make all the difference to our enjoyment of the presence of our Master, whether we have kept all His wishes or not. Even if there were only the faintest possibility of Believer's Baptism being His dear Will, I would be baptized, to be on the safe side. He will never find fault with those who did all they thought to be His will, even though they had slighter grounds for thinking so than we have for Believer's Baptism. He may find serious fault with those who did not investigate His commands for themselves, or postponed obedience, because the matter was non-essential. True love knows no distinction between the essential and the non-essential.

A Few Common Questions Answered

Is Believer's Baptism essential to Salvation? No; when our Lord Jesus died, He said "It is finished." And He meant that the Salvation of all who should trust Him was complete; and so the only thing now required of us is a simple heart-trust in Him. If you can look up into His face, and say, "Lord Jesus, I trust Thee," you are saved, though you have never been christened or baptized.

Why then need we be Baptized? Because our Lord Jesus wishes it. If there were only a dim suspicion that he wished it, it surely would be enough. Shall we do less for Him than the three mighty men did for David, when they risked their lives to get Him the water of childhood's well, for which He expressed a passing wish?

Supposing we were christened as Babes, need we be Baptized as Believers? Certainly; because christening does not fulfill all the conditions of baptism; christening was not your act at all; you did not do it; you cannot remember it; it was done for you. Besides in Acts xix. 1-6, there were some baptized a second time, when they learnt the truth about the Baptism of Christ.

Should we have our Children Christened? Why should you? Where is the scriptural warrant for it? The Blood of Christ is quite efficacious enough to save them if they die in childhood, without your adding a few drops of water. Will He, who said, "Suffer little children to come unto Me," cast a babe out of His heavenly home because it has not been sprinkled? The second Adam undid the results of the sin of the first Adam, and He undid them thoroughly, and completely, for all who do not refuse the benefits of His work by their wilful sin and neglect.

How can we live up to this high profession of the buried and risen life? There is only one way. Live a moment at a time; and each moment look to Jesus to make real your death to the old and sinful life, and your resurrection to a life in which all things are become new.

SELECTED TEXTS ON BAPTISM

Baptism shows forth our Burial and Resurrection with Christ. (Rom. i. 3-6.) (Col. ii. 12.)

Baptism is a *command,* but only to Believers.

Matt, xxviii. 18-19. Mark xvi. 15-16. Acts ii. 38.

Only Believers were baptized. Acts ii. 41. Acts x. 47-48.   "viii. 12.   "xvi. 14-15.   "viii. 13.   "xvi. 31-32-33.   "viii. 37-38.   "xviii. 8.   "ix. 17-18.   "xix. 5.

The *profession* made in Baptism is that of Death to Sin, and to the World, and of Resurrection to a new life of holiness unto God. (Rom. vi. 3-4).

There are only Three Households mentioned in Scripture as having been baptized.

1. — *That of the Jailer.* (Acts xvi. 33).

But to his household the Word was first spoken, (verse 32). And all of them, we are told, "were believing in God," (verse 34).

2,— *That of Stephanas.* (1 Cor. i. 16).

Of whose household it is said that they "addicted themselves to the ministry of the saints." (1 Cor. xvi. 15).

3. — *That of Lydia.* (Acts xvi. 15).

Regarding whose household we are given no particulars, but in all probability she was neither a wife nor a mother. Her household consisted of her assistants in the dyeing trade.

Baptism was not instituted *in the place* of Circumcision. The literal circumcision of the flesh was replaced, in the teachings of the Apostles, by the spiritual circumcision "made without hands." (Col. ii. 10.) "Circumcision," says St. Paul, is "that of the heart, in the spirit, and not in the letter." (Rom. ii. 29). There is not a word as to Baptism taking its place.

Baptism is nowhere spoken of in Scripture as a "Covenant," or "Sign in the flesh."

The *"New"* and *"Better"* Covenant, (Heb. viii. 6-13), is "In Christ's *blood*," (Luke xxii. 20), and *sealed* by His *death*. (Heb. ix. 15-16-17).

The Baptism of the *Spirit* does not do away with the necessity for the Baptism of *water,* but is a reason for it. (Acts x. 44-48).

"And now, why tarriest thou? arise, and be baptized."

The Stewardship of Money

THE blessed truth of consecration to the Lord Jesus is spreading among Christians, as dawn over the sky which it decks with opal and amethyst. And many are discovering the true law of their being in confessing themselves *the slaves of Jesus Christ.* The blood of His Cross was not only our expiation, but our purchase-money. We are not our own; we are bought with a price. Every throb of our pulse, every faculty of our nature, every possession that we hold, is not ours, but His. So that each of us may nail up over the door of our being the words which St. Paul uttered amid the dash of the storm, *"Whose I am, and whom I serve."*

But this sort of talk must be very carefully watched. If it is true, it is the most glorious position that a human being can assume, and it will make life one long summer day of blessedness. But if it is not true, then to use such expressions will soon cauterize the conscience and sere the heart. And it becomes us, O Christian souls, to take stock of ourselves now and again, and test ourselves, to see whether these words are simply pious expletives in which we lazily indulge or whether they embody the governing principle of our lives. An apostle may become an apostate if he trifle with holy things.

One of our commonest experiences is the handling of money. And nothing will sooner show whether our consecration be a reality or a sham, nor will anything serve more quickly to accentuate and enforce the life of consecration, than to spend our money daily beneath the sway of those principles, which it is so easy to enunciate and so difficult to practice.

We have no right to look on money as our absolute property. On every British coin in your possession you may read the letters D. G. (by the grace of God). Every coin is yours as the gift of God; as much so as if He had literally placed it in your open palm, saying, "Take this, my child, with your Father's love." The reasonableness of this is evident if we remember that all things owe their existence to the makership of God. "All that is in the heaven and in

74

the earth is Thine." "Thou hast created all things, for Thy pleasure they are and were created." "Both riches and honor come of Thee." And David was amply justified when, as the spokesman of his people, who had just made a marvelous offering for the house of the Lord, he said, *"Of Thine own have we given Thee."*

You tell me that you earn your money by the sweat of your brow. Every penny is the result of the putting forth of your muscular or mental power. Granted; but "thou shalt remember the Lord thy God; for it is He that giveth thee power to get wealth." He wards off paralyzing disease. He maintains the mind in perfect balance. Were He to touch the sinew of your strength, instantly you would become helpless to do another stroke to bring grist to the mill.

Besides, is it not our daily profession that we have devoted ourselves, with all we are and we have, to Him? Just as many a loving wife, richly dowered, prefers to have no distinction between her property and her husband's, and makes all over to his name, so we have professed to give ourselves and our all to Christ. We have taken His name, and our bank-books, our stocks and shares, our houses and businesses, have now written over them, in mystic characters, the initials of His name, the insignia of His glory, the brand-mark of His possession. Obviously, therefore, we have no right to look on our money as our absolute property. By our deed of gift it is His.

Is our daily practice on a level with this principle? It is a trick with little children, in a spasm of generosity, to give to those whom they love some dear possession, and to take it back again; or, at least, to use it without reference to the ownership they had conferred. And it is thus that too many Christians act toward Christ. They ask Him to consider all their possessions as His; but within an hour they are spending them as much their own as ever. They determine how much to give to a collection without once asking Him what He desires. They buy any extravagant knick-knack in a shop without considering that they have no right to spend His money in such things without an express warrant. They make their plans for the increase of their rent, for additional and needless outlay in their homes, and for some long and expensive excursion, without laying their suggestions before their Master to know His will. Either they ought never to have professed so much, or they are cultivating a habit of unreality, which will breed disaster to themselves and will bring shame upon their principles. If our money is really His, by His gift originally to us, and by our subsequent dedication to Him, surely He ought to have a voice in its expenditure. And the concession of that right to Him would speedily make our consecration real.

Do not suppose that it is your duty to give everything away. This would be an obvious mistake. It is our duty to provide for our own (1 Tim. v. 8) and to live in the sphere in which God has called us, and which in itself is a most precious talent (1 Cor. vii. 20). It is also clearly within our right to hold a certain amount as capital, for the increase of business and for the employment of labor. Capital may be as much considered the gift of God as any other of His gifts, and may be used for Him. And where a capitalist employs his property judiciously in furnishing work to others, taking no more of the profit than is the legitimate recompense of his time and knowledge and directing genius, and allowing his employees to share with him the common overplus; then, surely, that man is doing more real good in the world than if he gave away his property, distributing a pound each to as many poor families as he could find. But though I do not plead that consecrated Christians should give all away, I do insist upon it that they should regard all their money as Christ's, and spend every penny of it beneath His direction and in harmony with His will.

We are the Stewards of the Lord Jesus. This is His own comparison (Matt. xxv. 14). And it would be a happy thing if we could all come to look upon our several opportunities and faculties of doing good — power of speech, or thought, or writing, or the acquisition of money — in the same way as a faithful bailiff or steward looks on his master's goods.

May not the case be truly stated thus? Suppose that you are a man of large landed estates or other property. Circumstances compel you to go for an indefinite period beyond the seas. Before you go, you summon your steward, in whom you place implicit trust, and tell him that every quarter, when he has collected the rents and received the ordinary revenue, he may deduct from them the amount which he requires for the comfortable maintenance and education of his family, and for all needful expenditure; and that he shall expend the whole of the remainder for you, in helping some of your poor relations and in forwarding other projects in which you are interested. But in a short time you find, to your grief and astonishment, that, after you had left, the man whom you trusted suddenly launched out into an immense outlay on his house and equipage, on his servants and children, vying with the great ones of the land, and doling out a miserable pittance of 3*d.* per quarter to your relations, and of a guinea per year to your cherished institutions. Would you not feel that there had been a great breach of trust, and that instant steps should be taken to supersede the unfaithful steward in his stewardship? And yet is not this precisely the way in which many of us are treating our Lord's money to-day? Do we not use the bulk of it for ourselves, giving to Him and His work the chance coins which we may be able to spare or the subscriptions which we are obliged to give to maintain a character amongst our fellows? And there is therefore fulfilled with respect to us some ancient words, as true to-day as ever (Haggai i. 2; see also Malachi iii. 8-10). In how many houses and places of worship are those words being sadly verified!

What a contrast to this is supplied in the cases of others, living obscurely amongst us, but millionaires in the sight of Heaven! I have been credibly informed of one, whose income is $10,000 per annum, but who lives on $1,000 and administers $9,000 for the Lord's service; of another, whose income is $40,000, but who lives on $1,250 and gives away the remainder; of yet another, a governess, who, out of the $500 that she earns, keeps $250 and gives away the other half; while another who earns $7,500 lives on $500 and exercises a wise stewardship over the rest. A friend of my own, who has long since made a comfortable competence, is remaining in business for the purpose of devoting ail his profits to the cause of Christ. As surely as some have speaking or writing faculties, which they are bound to use for God's service, so others have business faculties, which they are equally required to exercise for the same purpose; not wrapping them to waste in the buried napkin. What would you think of a minister who ceased preaching for no other reason than that he had enough to live upon? And surely, if a man has no other talent than a business faculty, he had better go on employing that, rather than do nothing, for the Redeemer's glory.

There remain two or three simple rules, which may gather up into a practical shape the conclusions to which we have come.

1. — *Let us consecrate ourselves afresh to our Redeemer.* Let each reader of these words thoughtfully take that step which inspired David Livingstone in his mighty career! His last birthday but one was spent far away from home and friends, in the wild jungle, surrounded by those degraded Africans that lay so near his heart; and in his diary he penned these touching words: "My Jesus, My King, my Life, my All, I again dedicate my whole self to Thee." What better could you do than take your diary in hand, and write these very words? and, if you like, add an inventory of all that you include within their embrace; and then append your signature. Remember that scene in the churchyard of the Greyfriars, in Edinburgh, when the Covenanters signed their names in blood drawn from their hearts. Be as earnest as they were, and trust Christ to keep you true.

2. — *Determine beneath the eye of Christ how much you should legitimately spend on yourself.* There are several things to be considered, among the first of which is Life-insurance. Then rent, taxes, maintenance, education, and such-like. None of us can determine these things for another. They must be settled calmly under the Master's eye. Not in days of panic or pressure, for at such times we are not likely to form a correct estimate. But in times when we can quietly calculate what Christ would have us expend; always remembering that we have no right to presume on windfalls or miracles; or to provide for ostentation and excess; or to go beyond our income; or to risk running into debt. But when once we have prayerfully ascertained our position, we should maintain it, unless we have very clear tokens that we are to exchange it for another, whether better or worse. Many Christians, directly their income begins to increase, launch out into increased expenditure; whereas it may be that the increase is to be devoted to the cause of Christ. Ah! what moral ruin has come to families, because of the lavish waste of Christian homes! Other Christians, in times of straitness, begin to reduce *necessary* expenditure and to sell articles of use. It may be right to do so; but, on the whole, one would need to be clearly led by God's Spirit in all such matters. It

may be His will to maintain them as they are, but by other means until prosperity is restored to them. Our only care should be to please God, and never to run into debt. Leave the provision of each meal to Him who feeds the birds and clothes the flowers (Rom. xiii. 8 and Matt. vi. 25).

3. — *Give away a stated proportion of all you own or earn.* It may seem needless to insert this caution to those who should use all for Christ, but it is really most important, and for this reason: Our hearts are weak and fickle, and we are in danger of making so good a provision for ourselves that the Lord's surplus will be next to nothing. We remember so vividly the amount we give away that it bulks up largely beyond our mind; and we imagine that we are generous, until we see in figures how small a proportion our charity bears to our income. To guard against this, it is well always to put aside a certain part for the Lord before we begin to divide up the rest, so that His share may be as safe as our rent. This will not prevent us from still considering that the whole is His, or from administering the overplus for the furtherance of those objects that lie near His heart.

It is not within my province to say what proportion of our income we should statedly set apart for God. The patriarch gave a tenth; and surely the noon of Christianity should not inspire less benevolence than the twilight (Gen. xxviii. 22). And it has been calculated that the Jews gave in all at least one-fifth of their income to the maintenance of their religion. But of course the proportion we can statedly set apart for Christ must vary with our circumstances. A man, when his family is young, may be able to give only a tenth, who, when his expenses are less, can as easily dedicate a fifth or a third. Let each be fully persuaded in his own mind. Only let this principle be observed, that there be a stated proportion given out of every pound, whether the income be received weekly, or monthly, or quarterly, or whether it be only realized at the end of the year. Every business man knows pretty well what his income is, else how can he fix the sum given in for income tax? Let him deal as faithfully with God as with the Government officer; or let him expend during the current year a proportion of his income made during the previous one. So shall we obey the spirit at least of the Apostolic exhortation: "Upon the first day of the week let every one of you lay by him in store as God hath prospered him" (1 Cor. xvi. 2). When, then, we are called upon to give, it will be a luxury to administer wisely the Lord's money, and all the remainder will seem sanctified through the dedication of the first-fruits (Prov. iii. 9-10).

4. — *Sometimes let us make a special offering to the Lord Jesus.* We can only give Him what is His. And yet, though a wife has nothing of her own, she can make presents to her husband of what he gave her, and which she might have legitimately used for herself, but which she has saved until it grew into a worthy gift for her spouse. Love must give of that which costs her something. There are no gifts so precious in the eyes of the loved one as those which mean planning and self-sacrifice. And think you not that it delights the

heart of our Lord to receive at our hands love-tokens; precious ornaments and jewels; alabaster boxes, reserved once for self-adornment, but now gladly surrendered; articles of beauty and value, which we had hidden from the light of day, but which we present to Him, to show that our love is strong, personal, and self-forgetting? "He is worthy to receive riches." And the chief zest of such gifts is in their secrecy from all human eyes — a personal transaction between the Master and the loving heart. "That thine alms may be in secret."

5. — *Be careful to put the Lord's money aside.* We must not trust in our memories, or generalities. We must be minute, and specific, and careful, some having a bag, others a box, into which the Lord's portion is carefully put; some having a separate banking account; and all having some kind of ledger account, where we may put down what we receive and spend for Christ, that there may be no embezzlement, however inadvertent, of that which is not ours.

Of the rewards that will accrue we have no time to speak. Wasteful and harmful expenditure will be checked. Evil ways of getting money will be abandoned. Treasures will be laid up in the heavens. Bags which wax not old will be provided. The Lord's treasuries will be filled to overflowing. There will no longer be the sad refusal of young and eager hearts because there are no funds to send them forth to their coveted life-work in distant lands. The gulf between rich and poor will be bridged by many deeds of ministry and helpfulness. Whilst, better than all, the Master's voice will ring like music through the heart, "Well done, thou good and faithful servant; enter thou into the joy of thy Lord."

Don't Drift!

Yes, it is the *drifting* that is most to be feared. Men don't become atheists and swindlers at a leap. For every one who resolutely sets his face against God, there are hundreds who drift from Him.

An illustration occurred once in my own holiday experiences, which taught me to estimate fully the power of the tide to drift. We were staying on the coast of North Wales, and were desirous of visiting an island famous for its ruins and traditions. Nothing seemed easier than to cross the narrow straits which lay between it and the beach on which we stood. But as soon as we had got beyond the jutting headland, we found ourselves caught by a strong current, which persistently carried us out of our course, and would have drifted us, had we yielded to it, far down the coast. It took four of us four hours and a half of hard rowing to cross the straits which, with a flowing tide, we retraversed at night in about half an hour. Never since have I ignored the power of the current, so gentle, so imperceptible, so pleasant to yield to, so difficult to resist. And often have I been reminded of the episode, when I have seen young men drifting before the currents of moral influence on the great ocean of life.

Young men come up to our great centers of population from holy and blessed homes, where they have been born and bred. They are nice, amiable, well-meaning fellows, with no intention of going wrong, though perhaps with no very strong resolution to go right. The last words of advice from father or mother ring in their ears, urging them to keep up the good habits in which they had been trained from childhood; and they intend to conform to them.

If they fall in with a strong religious influence, it is not at all unlikely that all will turn out well. But if they go into some establishment or house where there is a fast, gay set, the Lord's day unkept, where filthy allusions pollute the talk, and gambling fills the leisure hours, after the first momentary shock is over they give themselves up to the strong prevailing current, and begin insensibly, but swiftly, to drift. It is not necessary at first that they should commit some flagrant sin; it is enough that *they cease to resist* the insidious influences around.

Young men, is this a true picture of your condition? If so, heed the advice of an elder brother, who has himself passed through city life, and who gathers up all the advice which he has to give in the words — *Don't drift!*

Don't drift into a loose way of keeping Sunday. When you are away from home you do not know where to go, what church to attend, what minister to hear. If you enter a place of worship, no one knows and perhaps no one welcomes you. You miss the familiar faces and voices of your childhood's earliest memories. You feel that your absence from that congregation, and indeed from any other, for the rest of the day would not be noticed, and so you stay away. Your pursuits may be quite innocent; and yet your absence from God's house, according to your olden practice, and without sufficient reason, is the first symptom of yielding to the swift current which urges you to drift.

My advice is to go to the several places of worship in the near neighborhood of your residence. Go once or twice to ascertain the character of the ministry and of the work carried on; and then attach yourselves to the one you find most helpful. Make for the minister direct, tell him who you are, whence you have come, and your intention of settling down in his congregation; and if he be a true man, he will be only too glad to welcome you. If he doesn't, I would advise you to betake yourself to some one who will.

When you settle in a new place, be sure also to find out the nearest Young Men's Christian Association; ask for the secretary, and he will introduce you to friends, and home, and many things young men want.

Don't drift into loose companionships. A man is made or marred by his friends. As fish take on the mottling of the ground on which they lie, and as butterflies resemble the flowers over which they hover, so do we become like those whom we choose for our companions. Don't drift into familiarity with any man till you are pretty sure of him, and have asked for God to show you his true character.

Beware of the man who goes in for a lot of showy jewelry, and professes to be able to show you a thing or two about life. He perhaps knows a little too much, and wants to see life at your expense. And when you have spent your last shilling, and he is tired of you, he will cast you off without mercy.

Beware of the man who talks slightingly of mother, father, home, or of women generally. Many men ridicule any allusion to the purity and tenderness of the home-circle, and apparently have no belief that woman can be other than the toy or victim of man — never his equal and confidante and friend. Beware of such men; the probability is that they have only lived to tempt the weaker sex, whom they now traduce; and that their vices have necessarily excluded them from the society of the pure and virtuous.

Beware of the man who professes himself too deeply versed in the science of the day to believe in the Bible, and who ridicules those who do. It is an easy thing to ask a question which might take days of teaching and investigation to answer. Destructive criticism is child's play. Any fool can fire a cathedral which would take centuries in building; and any street-arab may smash a window which neither modern wealth nor art can reconstruct. True wisdom is not destructive, but constructive. A man has no more right to steal away or spoil your faith than he has to deprive you of your eyesight or rob you of your purse. And if he attempt it, he betrays a dangerous character, of which you do well to beware.

Don't drift into extravagant expenditure. Better live on oatmeal porridge and brown bread, than spend more than you can afford or drift into debt. The pleasure of a day's outing or of an evening's gaiety has a nasty after -taste, when for weeks or months you have to avoid certain people because you owe them money which you cannot repay.

It is a temptation for us all to imitate the people above us in the social scale, but it is a miserable life to live, and very unsatisfactory, because we generally imitate their weaknesses and vices rather than their virtues. And yet it appears to afford much passing pleasure for the poor clerk to dress and speak with the airs of a young lord. One evening's conquest of the bar-maids and bar-loafers must be a rare luxury! But this kind of thing cannot be done without money. You cannot throw much money away out of a pound per week. And the result is, that a young man sometimes spends in a single evening money enough to fill his heart with anxiety for many a weary day, and is perhaps tempted to take money which does not belong to him, in order to stay pressing demands, and in hope of the opportunity of repayment, which never comes.

Don't drift into habits of gambling. There is plenty of it all around us; and a man feels rather lonely when he refuses to join in. I felt so some time ago on board an ocean-steamer, when I seemed to be nearly the only one that refused to join in a sweepstakes. The workshops and establishments are comparatively rare which are not filled with the buzz of excitement on the eve of some great race. And there are places in most large towns, clubs and such-like, where men have the opportunity of losing fortunes, if only they are fools enough.

It is not chiefly the love of money that urges men to bet, but the excitement of the chance, which relieves the monotony of their otherwise aimless existence. We can form no conception of the fascinations of this kind of life, as we look on them from without; just as we cannot realize the irresistible force of the whirlpool till we are being sucked into its gurgling vortex. But it is surely needless to fling ourselves into them to see what they are like. Once in, we shall probably find it impossible to get out. And we may get in almost imperceptibly. To deposit the first coin in a raffle or sweepstakes, to stake the first shilling on a horse, to lay a bet of a pair of gloves — these things may seem trifles, but they are a yielding to the outer rim of the whirlpool. Of course it is easy to break from them. But they may lead to other things, only removed from them by a single hair's-breadth, which will lead to others, and still others beyond. How much better to put the foot down and refuse the first! You mean to refuse the second; but if you are going to refuse at all, it will be unspeakably easier to refuse at first than afterwards.

Betting is a bad thing. It undoes society as the white ant the wooden houses of the tropics. Men who bet care for little else. Love and home are sacrificed to the companions of the betting-ring. Business is neglected, because they live in the feverish hope of coming in for a windfall, and of getting money without giving an equivalent of any sort.

Don't drift into habits of excessive drinking. Nothing is easier than to do this. The tides of strong drink are running swiftly through our streets, and every corner public-house is a jetty from which men may enter the boats and launch out upon the current. A few may enter it and yet escape. But for an enormous number there is little hope of escape, when once fairly afloat on the fascinating but perilous waters.

They say that smoking leads to drinking. If so, it would be well to avoid the first cigarette. Some of us have so many natural appetites to keep in order that we are thankful never to have awoke the habit of smoking, which seems a very masterful one, and terribly apt to become a tyrant. It would be foreign from my purpose to call smoking a sin. What right have I to add another to the ten commandments? But it certainly is to most people a "weight." In many cases it is the innocent little boy which, when once in the house, opens the door to a gang of thieves.

You are not specially a sinner, dear young fellow, because you smoke. But is it wise to begin a habit for which you cannot plead any good reason except that others do it, and which may lead you into drinking, bad companionships, and other things?

But other things drift a man into drinking habits. Loafing about the streets in the evenings; drinking beer without at the same time eating solid victuals; standing treat to your companions, because you want to look large in their esteem, and with the certainty that you will have to drink what they provide in return; doing business over a wine-bar; spending your evenings in places like music-halls, where drink passes round, and where the proprietor looks shyly on those who don't patronize the buffet — all these are easy methods of drifting into drink. No man means to be a drunkard when he starts drinking. Those who are now in the agony of delirium were once as pure and true as you; but they were carried down an almost insensible gradient. Beware of their fate, and don't follow their earlier steps, lest you acquire a momentum you cannot arrest, and go down to hell. There is no better safeguard to a young man in life than the pledge of total abstinence. He perhaps may not sign a pledge at a meeting, but he can write one in his own chamber, and resolve, by God's help, never to touch this accursed foe of human hearts and happiness and homes.

Don't drift into habits of impurity. In us all there are appetites and desires which are beautiful and innocent enough when kept in their right place; but they are very reluctant to be kept there, and are ever chafing to ascend the throne of the being and assume the mastership of the life. It is pleasant to allow them thus to ascend, but who shall depict the horrors of the wreckage of all that is bright and beautiful and happy in the life of the miserable victim who has yielded to their first suggestions?

Beware of drifting into secret sins, witnessed by no eye but God's. Beware of the society of those who are familiar with the ways of darkness and impurity. Beware of spectacles and pictures, of amusements and books, that excite the lower passions. Never go to a place to which you could not take your mother or sister. Never get familiar with a girl whom you could not introduce to the purest woman you know. Never treat a girl in another way than you would like a man to treat your own sister.

It is not necessary to yield to temptation. Abstinence from strong drink and excessive animal food; plenty of gymnastic, cycling, and muscular exercise; hard mattresses, cold bathing, early rising, will answer many of the questions which so often perplex young men. And there is better than all — the power and purity of Jesus, which you may claim and use in all moments of need. One earnest, believing cry for help will bring Him near. And when He enters the soul impurity can no more stand against His indwelling than straw before fire, or darkness before day.

Don't drift into an imprudent marriage. It is well when a young man meets a good girl. I never object to an early engagement when the couple are well-mated, though I would urge a deferred marriage until the comforts of a home can be provided either by the love of friends or by the results of united savings. And no home is so sweet as that which has been chosen and furnished by the taste and self-denial of those who are to enter it.

You ought not to choose your life-partner only from seeing her in evening dress or in company. All sweet faces do not tell a perfectly true story of the inner temper. You need a wife who knows something more than how to play one or two set pieces on the piano or sing half a dozen songs. The girl who understands all the details of household management, who knows how all should be done though she may never have to do it, who has been good to her parents and younger brothers and sisters, who dresses simply and neatly, who knows how to make a shilling do a shilling's work, who is deeply religious — that is the kind of woman who will make a good wife; and till God sends her to you don't flirt or play with a girl's affections or lead any to think that you care for them when you don't.

Don't drift into a mere money-making machine. Some seem to live for nothing else than add a few more coins to their rising pile; and to do this they sacrifice all that makes life sweet and noble and honorable. Have a lofty aim. Spend your life for the best results. Be more eager to get *up* than to get *on*. There is no harm in ambition when it is directed to doing the best you can to make the world better and those around you happier; but it is a detestable passion to seek money for money's sake. Your aim must be to seek first the things that make for righteousness and peace, for God's glory and man's good. Be faithful in these, in your small sphere, and it will be almost certain that you will be put into a position where you will have the chance of being faithful also in much.

You tell me that you cannot resist the strong current on which you are already launched, and that you have already commenced to drift. But it is not too late. Send up a cry of distress to the Lord Jesus, asking Him to come on board your boat. He is stronger than the mightiest current. And then, if you like to put it so, give Him the towing-line, that he may take it in His hand and tow you up the strong stream to His own bright Home.

There is no better policy, dear young brother, than to give your heart to Jesus. Take Him as your Saviour, Master, and Friend. Ask Him to live in your soul, making you pure and sweet and strong. Follow Him in His footsteps of self-sacrifice for the sake of others. Go to no place where you cannot take Him also. Let His friends be yours, and see that yours are His. Ask Him to put you in that position where you can please and glorify Him best; and also remember that prayer and waiting will untie the stoutest knots and unravel the greatest difficulties.

Why Sign the Pledge?

THE feeling in favor of Total Abstinence from Strong Drink is rapidly growing in our beloved motherland. By the efforts and self-sacrifice of tens of thousands, a strong public sentiment is being formed, like a mighty Breakwater. An arrest is being placed on the onward march of drunkenness; and many a bark, battered by the fury of Passion and Self-indulgence, is safely moored in the haven, sheltered from utter ruin, and able to repair its terrible wreckage. Happy are we who live in such a time. Let us do our best to build our few stones into this great Breakwater, which is only made up by the small work of unknown and soon-forgotten builders.

One important means by which so much has been done has been the use of the Pledge. Humanly speaking, if it had not been for the Pledge, the present sentiment in favor of Total Abstinence would not have been possible. And it will be a great mistake if the signing of the Pledge should ever fall into disuse or become an object of contempt. We must not kick away the ladder by which we have climbed up.

And yet in some quarters there is a disposition to think and speak lightly of the Pledge. "Oh," says one, "I can keep teetotal without signing your Pledge." "Yes," says another, "it is childish to sign away your freedom." "It may be all very well," says a third, "for some to do it, but it is not so for me."

Why, then, should we sign the Pledge of Total Abstinence?

Sign the Pledge: it is your protest against Strong Drink. It is time for every thoughtful person to enter a solemn protest against Strong Drink, which, every year, is inflicting such awful havoc among our race. Who can be indifferent to the woes it brings on hearts and homes, on villages and towns, on countries and continents? Well may the Hindoos call it "Shame-water." There is not a house in which you may not find its slain. There is not a newspaper that does not record its diabolical outrages. There is not a public officer that could not bear damning evidence against it. England can never be the "Merrie England" of olden times till Drink has been dethroned. We cannot do much, but let us do what we can. We have a voice, a right to cry aye or nay, a power to assent or protest. Let us use them by all means on the right side. And if we cannot express our feelings in any other way, let us at least sign a solemn declaration on paper that we will never again touch the cruellest foe that ever revelled in human tears and blood.

Sign the Pledge: it will benefit your health. Alcohol is not more necessary to health than any other chemical or medicinal agent. It excites the heart, hinders digestion, disturbs the liver, and stupefies the brain. It gives a momentary glow and stimulus, but you have to pay for them afterward by an inevitable lessening of vital heat, and animal power, and mental force. Even in moderate quantities it acts as an irritant and a poison. The athlete, in training for a boat-race, a prize-fight, or a running match, must absolutely forego the use of Alcohol; and if men do not want it for such extraordinary exertions, why do you want it for ordinary ones? Our recent expeditions in Abyssinia, the Transvaal, and Egypt prove that if a General wishes his troops to perform forced marches, or to undergo unusual fatigues, he must substitute coffee for grog. The extremes of the Arctic circle and the Tropical sun are best endured on cold water, as the experience of many explorers and travelers proves. The tables of Insurance Offices show that 100 moderate drinkers die for every 73 abstainers, and many offices have a special section, to give abstainers the benefits of insurance at a less price. It would be a perfect revelation to some of you who read these words if you would give Total Abstinence a trial; your appetite would be better, your minds would be clearer, your nerves would be stronger, and your whole system would get fitness and tone.

Sign the Pledge: it will save your time. We have only one short life to live, and we cannot afford to fling the diamond moments into the rushing stream beside us. How many days in the fore-part of the week are spent by our working-classes in public-houses, which are a dead loss to them, and their families, and the country! How many hours are spent by clerks and commercial travelers, in the course of the week, at the bars of railway stations and restaurants, which might be sown with the seeds of golden harvest! How many evenings are worse than wasted in convivial company, which might be spent in innocent and health-giving recreation, or in acquiring knowledge which would unlock many a shut door! From all this you would escape if you signed the Pledge.

Sign the Pledge: it will save your purse. Sit down and calculate how much you spend per day in Drink, not only for yourself, but also for those whom you treat. It will amount to a respectable sum in the course of the year. Add to this the money you might earn in the time you now lose. Add to this all the sums squandered wastefully in the company into which habits of drinking lead you. And when all is put together, would it not make a nice nest-egg against a rainy day, or for illness and old age? I often say to those who sign my Pledge-cards that there is a $500 Banknote hidden inside the double card-board.

Sign the Pledge: it will save you from temptation. You have no intention of becoming a Drunkard; you scorn the thought. But there is a risk of your becoming one, so long as you tamper with the Drink. You take it now for the sake of society, but you will come to take it for its own sake. You cannot be sure that daily dram-drinking may not do for you what it has done for myriads, in exciting a thirst, now perhaps dormant, but which, when once aroused, will be unsatiable! Wise men, good men, strong men have been mastered by that awful thirst, who no more expected such a thing than you do. Is it not folly, then, for you to run the risk of creating it? Why not stop at once, before that thirst has been aroused?

You tell me that it seems hard for you to do without the Drink. Then *that* is a sure sign that the accursed appetite has got a foothold within you. Spring off the car ere it rushes down the incline. Run the boat into a creek ere it is caught by the rapids above the falls. Force the cloven foot back out of the door before the demon has time to thrust his whole body into your heart and life. Do it at once. Do it now. You ask not to be led into temptation, then don't go into it. Public-houses are well-called "shades" and "vaults": they are the shades of death, and vaults for the burial of all that is noblest and best in men. Avoid them. Pass them by. Refuse to enter them unless the Good Shepherd sends you there to find a lost sheep.

Sign the Pledge: it will make a definite starting point in your history. In all efforts after a better life it is well to have some landmark or time-mark, to which to look back and from which to date. There is a sort of satisfaction in being able to point to a mental stone-cairn, or crease-line, or white-painted post, standing out on the moorland of life, and to say, "Up to that point I lived a selfish, evil life, but since then I have tried to run fair and well, by the help of God.".

With some it is a sermon; with others it is a birthday, a death, an entry in the diary, or a New Year's Eve; with others it is the visit of some Gospel Temperance Advocate to their town. But in many cases the same purpose is served by signing the Pledge. The date of that Pledge-card is a birthday, a new start, a beginning of a new era in the story of the soul; and it very often leads to the second step of Faith in Christ.

Sign the Pledge: it makes a strong obligation. When a man gives up the Drink, he must do all that can be done to strengthen his resolution. If he simply makes a resolution, he feels at liberty to withdraw from it if he choose. But if he double-knots his resolution with a solemn promise to which he has put his hand, then he feels bound by the most solemn obligations. He cannot think of breaking his word. Pie dare not violate his plighted troth. And in the moment of temptation, his self-respect, his love for truth, his desire to be a man of his word, his written vow, will be a strong reason for saying No.

A gentlemen who signed the Pledge-card recently, said that during the whole of the next day he carried it in his pocket, and took it out fifteen times to remind him that he had put his hand to a promise which he dared not violate, and could not retract.

Sign the Pledge: it will give a sufficient answer to those who tempt you to drink. There is no answer that a man can give so good as this. If he refuses because he is hot, he will be advised to drink to get cool. If he refuses because he is cold, he will be recommended to drink to get warm. If he refuses because he cannot afford it, his companions will gladly treat him. If he refuses because he is not well, there is no ailment to which flesh is heir for which intoxicating drinks are not prescribed as a certain cure. Men who are well, drink till they are ill; and then drink to get themselves well again, none of these excuses avail, but if a man says, "I have signed the Pledge," they may think him a fool, but they cannot say that he has not given a sufficient reason; and if they are true men themselves, they dare not ask him to break his word. If a man asks you to drink after you have signed the Pledge, he is no true friend; he is doing the devil's work. He is certain to turn round and insult you after you have done his will, because he will have lost the last fragment of respect for you.

There are some men who must have a reason to give others for doing as they do; here at least is a clear, straightforward, intelligible reason, which puts an end to controversy, and settles the matter forever — "I have signed the Pledge."

Sign the Pledge: it keeps it from becoming the badge of a reclaimed drunkard. If the Pledge were only signed by men who had been drunkards, but who were trying to live a new life, it would become the badge of reclaimed drunkards, and it would soon cease to be signed by this class of men, who need it most. This would be a great calamity.

"I dare not sign the Pledge," said a young doctor to a friend who was trying to get him to do so, as a means of saving him from ruin. "Why not?" was his friend's reply. "Because if people heard that I had done so they would say that there must have been a screw loose in my character, and that I was a reclaimed drunkard." "No," said his friend, "they never can say that, for it has been signed by thousands of thousands on whose character there has never been a stain." The answer re-assured him; he signed the Pledge, and is now an earnest Christian worker in one of our large towns.

You may not need to sign the Pledge for yourself, but sign it that you may give it the benefit, the weight, the standing of your own moral character. If everyone of reputable and stainless character were to stand aloof, the Pledge would be a hopeless failure. Every respectable Christian person who signs it is like one of the corks floating on the surface of the sea, helping to sustain the heavy nets laden with fish.

Sign the Pledge: it makes it easier for others to do the same. We are creatures of fashion. We cannot help it. We are made so. What one does, the others are apt to do. There's many an eager eye looking to see what the reader of these lines is going to do; if he signs the Pledge, that boy, that companion, that servant, will do the same; but if he refuses to do so, it may be that that waiting one will also refuse, and that refusal will lead to ruin.

More eyes are watching us than we think. More lives than we know are on the balance, waiting for the feather of our example to turn them this way or that. Are we right in leaving anything undone that might save one for whom Christ died? We must use all means to save some, though the use of the means compel us to forego some boasted liberty, or some loved indulgence.

Don't say that you have no influence, it is only an excuse; you have; you would not like another to say that. "I have no influence," said a man to one who asked him to take the Pledge for the sake of others. His wife came up at that moment and said, "That's true, you have no more influence than a cat." If you say that again, woman," said he, "I will knock you down." Of course you have influence; use it well.

Sign the Pledge: it will win you friends. We all need friends, and if we have given up those who gather around the Drink, we need others, and we are most likely to find these wherever there are Pledge-cards to be had for signature. It is all very well to resolve to give up the Drink and to keep the vow secretly, but it is much better to take the Pledge in the presence of one or more persons, who shall bear witness to what they have seen, and who will be bound to you in the bonds of a new and common brotherhood, because they have done the same thing, and are pledged to the same cause.

But I do not like to sign away my liberty. Then, if you are unmarried, you will never be married; you will surely never promise to love and honor any one individual, because you may want to change your mind. And what is true in this case is true in others, and is a sufficient answer to the objection. If you like, take the Pledge *for a short time only*, as you take the lease of a house; you can easily renew it again and again. Or, better still, promise to abstain, by God's help, from all intoxicating Drinks, as a Beverage, *until you return your Pledge-card to the friend from whom you have received it.* This will give you an opportunity of relinquishing it when you choose, and it will give him an opportunity of speaking earnestly with you when your purpose is faltering.

But I may be forced to drink. If you are, you will not violate your Pledge. You only promise to abstain from Intoxicants *as a Beverage*. If it is poured down your throat by force, or when you are fainting; if the physician compels you to take it; if you take it unawares in some dish of cookery: your Pledge is not broken. It is not you that break it.

But I have taken it, and broken more than once. Then take it again, in humble dependence on the Saviour, "who has been manifested to destroy the works of the devil." Most, if not all, Total Abstinence Pledges lay stress on the words, God Helping Me. These words are the heart of all. If they are not felt deep down in the soul the Pledge is not good for much, it rests on mere human strength. But when God is appealed to, the case is altered. Divine power pours into the spirit which is lifted up to Him in prayer and trust. Angel hands are stretched out to hold back the erring feet. A holy garrison is put inside the weak and trembling nature to hold it against the foe. Ask the Lord Jesus to forgive the past. Ask Him to save you from your enemy. Ask Him to shield you in the day of battle. Ask Him, when the door is nearly battered in, to put His foot against it and keep it closely shut. He is able to keep you from stumbling. He is able to keep that which you commit to Him. He is able to make you more than a conqueror. Put yourself into His hands before you leave your room in the morning. Keep looking to Him all day. Praise Him for His grace each night.

"What's that, that you keep mumbling to yourself?" said a working-man to another at a little distance from him in the same shop. "I keep on saying, 'Lord help me,'" was the reply; "I say it day and night; it is the only way I know of to keep down my thirst for the Drink."

Take heart, my friend; the battle may be sharp, but victory is sure. And when once you stand firm on the rock, be on the alert to rescue others from the raging waters of Strong Drink.

Where am I Wrong?

THIS is thy eager question, O Christian soul, and thy bitter complaint. On the faces and in the lives of others who are known to thee, thou hast discerned a light, a joy, a power, which thou enviest with a desire that oppresses thee, but for which thou shouldest thank God devoutly. It is well when we are dissatisfied with the low levels on which we have been wont to live, and begin to ask the secret of a sweeter, nobler, more victorious life. The sleeper who turns restlessly is near awaking, and will find that already the light of the morning is shining around the couch on which slumber has been indulged too long. "Awake, thou that sleepest, and arise from the dead, and Christ shall give thee light."

We must, however, remember that *temperaments differ*. Some seem born in the dark, and carry with them through life an hereditary predisposition to melancholy. Their nature is set to a minor key and responds most easily and naturally to depression. They look always on the dark side of things, and in the bluest of skies discover the cloud no bigger than a man's hand. Theirs is a shadowed pathway, where glints of sunshine strike feebly and with difficulty through the dark foliage above.

Such a temperament may be thine; and if it be, thou never canst expect to obtain just the same exuberant gladness which comes to others, nor must thou complain if it is so. This is the burden which thy Saviour's hands shaped for thee, and thou must carry it for Him, not complaining, or parading it to the gaze of others, or allowing it to master thy steadfast and resolute spirit, but bearing it silently, and glorifying God amid all. But, though it may be impossible to win the joyousness which comes to others, there may at least be rest, and victory, and serenity — Heaven's best gifts to man.

We must remember, also, that *emotion is no true test of our spiritual state*. Rightness of heart often shows itself in gladness of heart, just as bodily health generally reveals itself in exuberant spirits. But it is not always so. In other words, absence of joy does not always prove that the heart is wrong. It may do so, but certainly not invariably. Perhaps the nervous system may have been overtaxed, as Elijah's was in the wilderness, when, after the long strain of Carmel and his flight was over, he lay down upon the sand and asked to die — a request which God met, not with rebuke, but with food and sleep. Perhaps the Lord has withdrawn the light from the landscape in order to see whether He was loved for Himself or merely for His gifts. Perhaps the discipline of life has culminated in a Gethsemane, where the bitter cup is being placed to the lips by a Father's hand, though only a Judas can be seen, and in the momentary anguish caused by the effort to renounce the will it is only possible to lie upon the ground, with strong crying and tears, which the night wind bears to God. Under such circumstances as these exuberant joy is out of place. Somber colors become the tried and suffering soul. High spirits would be as unbecoming here as gaiety in the home shadowed by death. Patience, courage, faith are the suitable graces to be manifested at such times.

But, when allowance is made for all these, it is certain that many of us are culpably missing a blessedness which would make us radiant with the light of Paradise; and the loss is attributable to some defect in our character which we shall do well to detect and make right.

1. — Perhaps you do not Distinguish between your Standing and your Experience. Our experiences are fickle as April weather; now sunshine, now cloud; lights and shadows chasing each other over miles of heathery moor or foam-flecked sea. But our standing in Jesus changes not. It is like Himself — the same yesterday, to-day, and forever. It did not originate in us, but in His everlasting love, which, foreseeing all that we should be, loved us notwithstanding all. It has not been purchased by us, but by His precious blood, which pleads for us as mightily and successfully when we can hardly claim it as when our faith is most buoyant. It is not maintained by us, but by the Holy Spirit. If we have fled to Jesus for salvation, sheltering under Him, relying on Him, and trusting Him, though with many misgivings, as well as we may, then we are one with Him forever. We were one with Him in the grave; one with Him on the Easter morn; one with Him when He sat down at God's right hand. We are one with Him now as He stands in the light of His Father's smile, as the limbs of the swimmer are one with the head, though it alone is encircled with the warm glory of the sun, while they are hidden beneath the waves. And no doubt or depression can for a single moment affect or alter our acceptance with God through the blood of Jesus, which is an eternal fact.

You have not realized this, perhaps, but have thought that your standing in Jesus was affected by your changeful moods. As well might the fortune of a ward in chancery be diminished or increased by the amount of her spending money. Our standing in Jesus is our invested capital, our emotions at the best are but our spending money, which is ever passing through our pocket or purse, never exactly the same. Cease to consider how you feel, and build on the immovable rock of what Jesus is, and has done, and is doing and will do for you, world without end.

2. — Perhaps you Live too much in your Feelings, too little in your Will. We have no direct control over our feelings, but we have over our will. "Our wills are ours, to make them Thine." God does not hold us responsible for what we *feel,* but for what we *will.* In His sight we are not what we feel, but what we will. Let us, therefore, not live in the summerhouse of emotion, but in the central citadel of the will, wholly yielded and devoted to the will of God.

At the Table of the Lord, the soul is often suffused with holy emotion, the tides rise high, the tumultuous torrents of joy knock loudly against the floodgates as if to beat them down, and every element in the nature joins in the choral hymn of rapturous praise. But the morrow comes, and life has to be faced in the grimy counting-house, the dingy shop, the noisy factory, the godless workroom; and as the soul compares the joy of yesterday with the difficulty experienced in walking humbly with the Lord, it is inclined to question whether it is quite so devoted and consecrated as it was. But, at such a time, how fair a thing it is to remark that the wall has not altered its position by a hair's breadth, and to look up and say: "My God, the spring-tide of emotion has passed away like a summer brook; but in my heart of hearts, in my will. Thou knowest I am as devoted, as loyal, as desirous to be only for Thee, as in the blessed moment of unbroken retirement at Thy feet." This is an offering with which God is well pleased. And thus we may live a calm, peaceful life.

3. — Perhaps you have Disobeyed some clear Command. Sometimes a soul comes to its spiritual adviser, speaking thus:

"I have no conscious joy, and have had but little for years."

"Did you once have it?"

"Yes, for some time after my conversion to God."

"Are you conscious of having refused obedience to some distinct command, which came into your life, but from which you shrank?"

Then the face is cast down, and the eyes film with tears, and the answer comes with difficulty.

"Yes, years ago I used to think that God required a certain thing of me; but I felt I could not do what He wished, was uneasy for some time about it, but after a while it seemed to fade from my mind, and now it does not often trouble me."

"Ah, soul, that is where thou hast gone wrong, and thou wilt never get right till thou goest right back through the weary years to the point where thou didst drop the thread of obedience, and performest that one thing which God demanded of thee so long ago, but on account of which thou didst leave the narrow track of implicit obedience."

Is not this the cause of depression to thousands of Christian people? They are God's children, but they are disobedient children. The Bible rings with one long demand for obedience. The key-word of the Book of Deuteronomy is. *Observe and Do*. The burden of the Farewell Discourse is, *If ye love Me, keep My commandments*. We must not question or reply or excuse ourselves. We must not pick and choose our way. We must not take some commands and reject others. We must not think that obedience in other directions will compensate for disobedience in some one particular. God gives us one command at a time, borne in upon us, not in one way only, but in many; by this He tests us. If we obey in this, He will flood our soul with blessing and lead us forward into new paths and pastures. But if we refuse in this, we shall remain stagnant and water-logged, make no progress in Christian experience, and lack both power and joy.

4. — Perhaps you are Permitting some Known Evil. When water is left to stand the particles of silt betray themselves, as they fall one by one to the bottom. So if you are quiet you may become aware of the presence in your soul of permitted evil. Dare to consider it. Do not avoid the sight as the bankrupt avoids his tell-tale ledgers or as the consumptive patient the stethoscope. Compel yourself quietly to consider whatever evil the Spirit of God discovers to your soul. It may have lurked in the cupboards and cloisters of your being for years, suspected but unjudged. But whatever it be, and whatever its history, be sure that it has brought the shadow over your life which is your daily sorrow.

Does your will refuse to relinquish a practice or habit which is alien to the will of God?

Do you permit some secret sin to have its unhindered way in the house of your life?

Do your affections roam unrestrained after forbidden objects?

Do you cherish any resentment or hatred toward another, to whom you refuse to be reconciled?

Is there some injustice which you refuse to forgive, some charge which you refuse to pay, some wrong which you refuse to confess?

Are you allowing something yourself which you would be the first to condemn in others, but which you argue may be permitted in your own case, because of certain reasons with which you attempt to smother the remonstrances of conscience?

In some cases the hindrance to conscious blessedness lies not in sins, but in *weights* which hang around the soul. Sin is that which is always and everywhere wrong; but a weight is any thing which may hinder or impede the Christian life, without being positively sin. And thus a thing may be a weight to one which is not so to another. Each must be fully persuaded in his own mind. And wherever the soul is aware of its life being hindered by the presence of any one thing, then, however harmless in itself, and however innocently permitted by others, there can be no alternative, but it must be cast aside as the garments of the lads when, on the village green, they compete for the prize of the wrestle or the race.

5. — Perhaps you Look too much Inwards on Self, instead of Outwards on the Lord Jesus. The healthiest people do not think about their health; the weak induce disease by morbid introspection. If you begin to count your heart-beats, you will disturb the rhythmic action of the heart. If you continually imagine a pain anywhere, you will produce it. And there are some true children of God who induce their own darkness by morbid self-scrutiny. They are always going back on themselves, analyzing their motives, reconsidering past acts of consecration, comparing themselves with themselves. In one form or another self is the pivot of their life, albeit that it is undoubtedly a religious life. What but darkness can result from such a course? There are certainly times in our lives when we must look within, and judge ourselves, that we be not judged. But this is only done that we may turn with fuller purpose of heart to the Lord. And when once done, it needs not to be repeated. "Leaving the things behind" is the only safe motto. The question is. not whether we did as well as we might, but whether we did as well as we could at the time.

We must not spend all our lives in cleaning our windows, or in considering whether they are clean, but in sunning ourselves in God's blessed light. That light will soon show us what still needs to be cleansed away, and will enable us to cleanse it with unerring accuracy. Our Lord Jesus is a perfect reservoir of everything the soul of man requires for a blessed and holy life. To make much of Him, to abide in Him, to draw from Him, to receive each moment from His fallness, is therefore the only condition of soul-health. But to be more concerned with self than with Him is like spending much time and thought over the senses of the body and never using them for the purpose of receiving impressions from the world outside. Look off unto Jesus. Delight thyself in the Lord. My soul, wait thou only upon God!

6. — Perhaps you spend too little Time in communion with God through His Word. It is not necessary to make long prayers, but it is essential to be much alone with God; waiting at His door; hearkening for His voice; lingering in the garden of Scripture for the coming of the Lord God in the dawn or cool of the day. No number of meetings, no fellowship with Christian friends, no amount of Christian activity can compensate for the neglect of the still hour.

When you feel least inclined for it, there is most need to make for your closet with the shut door. Do for duty's sake what you cannot do as a pleasure, and you will find it become delightful. You can better thrive without nourishment than become happy or strong in Christian life without fellowship with God.

When you cannot pray for yourself, begin to pray for others. When your desires flag, take the Bible in hand, and begin to turn each text into petition; or take up the tale of your mercies and begin to translate each of them into praise. When the Bible itself becomes irksome, inquire whether you have not been spoiling your appetite by sweetmeats and renounce them; and believe that the Word is the wire along which the voice of God will certainly come to you, if the heart is hushed and the attention fixed. "I will hear what God the Lord shall speak."

More Christians than we can count are suffering from a lack of prayer and Bible study, and no revival is more to be desired than that of systematic private Bible study. There is no short and easy method of godliness which can dispense with this.

7. — Perhaps you have never given Yourself entirely over to the Mastership of the Lord Jesus. We are His by many ties and rights, but too few of ns recognize his lordship. We are willing enough to take Him as Saviour; we hesitate to make Him King. We forget that God has exalted Him to be Prince as well as Saviour. And the Divine order is irreversible. Those who ignore the lordship of Jesus cannot build up a strong or happy life.

Put the sun in its central throne, and all the motions of the planets assume a beautiful order. Put Jesus on the throne of the life, and all things fall into harmony and peace. Seek first the kingdom of God, and all things are yours. Consecration is the indispensable condition of blessedness.

So shall the light break on thy path, such as has not shone there for many days. Yea, "thy sun shall no more go down, neither shall thy moon withdraw herself; but the Lord shall be unto thee an everlasting light, *and the days of thy mourning shall be ended.*"

Our Bible Reading

THE whole of Christian Livings in my opinion, hinges on the way in which Christian people read the Bible for themselves. All sermons and addresses, all Bible-readings and classes, all religious magazines and books, can never take the place of our own quiet study of God's precious Word. We may measure our growth in grace by the growth of our love for private Bible study. And we may be sure that there is something seriously wrong when we lose our appetite for the Bread of Life. Perhaps we have been eating too many sweets; or taking too little exercise; or breathing too briefly in the bracing air, which sweeps over the uplands of Spiritual Communion with God.

Happy are they who have learnt the blessed art of discovering for themselves the treasures of the Bible, which are hidden just a little below the surface, so as to test our real earnestness in finding them. No specimens are so interesting as those which the Naturalist has obtained by his own exertions, and each of which has a history. No flowers are so fragrant as those which we discover for ourselves, nestling in some woodland dell, remote from the eye and step of men. No pearls are so priceless as those which he have sought for ourselves in the calm, clear depths of the ocean of truth. Only those who know it can realize the joy that fills the spirit when one has made a great "find" in some hidden connection, some fresh reference, or some railway lines from verse to verse.

There are a few simple rules, which may help many more to acquire this holy art, and I venture to note them down. May the Holy Spirit Himself own and use them!

1. — *Make time for Bible Study.* The Divine Teacher must have fixed and uninterrupted hours for meeting His scholars. His Word must have our freshest and brightest thoughts. We must give Him our best, and the first-fruits of our days. Hence there is no time for Bible study like the early morning. For we cannot give such undivided attention to the holy thoughts that glisten like diamonds on its pages after we have opened our letters, glanced through the paper, and joined in the prattle of the breakfast table. The manna had to be gathered before the dew was off and the sun was up; otherwise it melted.

We ought, therefore, to aim at securing at least half an hour before breakfast for the leisurely and loving study of the Bible. To some this may seem a long time in comparison with what they now give, but it will soon seem all too short. The more you read the Bible the more you will want to read it. It is an appetite which grows as it is fed. And you will be well repaid. The Bible seldom speaks, and certainly never its deepest, sweetest words, to those who always read it in a hurry. Nature can only tell her secrets to such as will sit still in her sacred Temple till their eyes lose the glare of earthly glory and their ears are attuned to her voice. And shall Revelation do what Nature cannot? Never. The man who shall win the blessedness of hearing her must watch daily at her gates and wait at the posts of her doors. There is no chance for a lad to grow who only gets an occasional mouthful of food and always swallows that in a hurry!

Of course this season before breakfast is not possible for all. The Invalid; the Nurse with broken rest; the Public Servant, whose night is often turned into day — these stand alone, and the Lord Jesus can make it up to them, sitting with them at mid-day, if needs be, beside the well. In the case of such as can only snatch a few words of Scripture as they hasten to their work, there will be repeated the miracle of the manna. "He that gathered much had nothing over;" i.e. all we get in our morning reading is not too much for the needs of the day; "and he that gathered little had no lack;" i.e., when, by force of circumstances, we are unable to do more than snatch up a hasty handful of manna, it will last us all through the day; the cruse of oil shall not waste, and the barrel of meal shall not fail.

It would be impossible to name all who have traced their usefulness and power to this priceless habit. Sir Henry Havelock always spent the first two hours of each day alone with God; and if the encampment was struck at 6 a.m., he would rise at 4. Earl Cairns rose daily at 6 o'clock to secure an hour and a half for the study of the Bible and for prayer, before conducting family worship at a quarter to 8, even when the late hours of the House of Commons left him not more than two hours for his night's rest. It is the practice of a beloved friend, who stands in the front rank of modern Missionaries, to spend at least three hours each morning with his Bible; and he has said that he often puts aside pressing engagements, that he may not only have time, but be fresh for it.

There is no doubt a difficulty in awakening and arising early enough to get time for our Bibles before breakfast. But these difficulties present no barrier to those who must get away early for daily business or for the appointments of pleasure. If we mean to get up, we can get up. Of course we must prepare the way for early-rising by retiring early to obtain our needed rest, though it be at the cost of some cosy hours by the fireside in the winter's night. But with due forethought and fixed purpose the thing can surely be done. "All things are possible to him that believeth."

I never shall forget seeing Charles Studd, early one November morning, clothed in flannels to protect him from the cold, and rejoicing that the Lord had awaked him at 4 a.m. to study His commands. He told me then that it was his custom to trust the Lord to call him and enable him to rise. Might not we all do this? The weakest can do all things through Christ that strengtheneth us. And though you have failed again and again when you have trusted your own resolutions, you cannot fail when you are simply trusting Him. "He wakeneth me morning by morning." "He took him by the right hand and lifted him up; and immediately his feet and ankle bones received strength."

2. — *Look up for the Teaching of the Holy Spirit.* No one can so well explain the meaning of his words as lie who wrote them. Tennyson could best explain some of his deeper references in "In Memoriam." If, then, you want to read the Bible as you should, make much of the Holy Ghost, who inspired it through holy men. As you open the book, lift up your heart, and say: "Open Thou mine eyes, that I may behold wondrous things out of Thy law. Speak, Lord, for Thy servant heareth."

It is marvelous what slender light commentaries cast on the inner meaning of Scripture. A simple-hearted believer, depending on the aid of the Holy Ghost, will find things in the Bible which the wisest have mistaken or missed. Well might St. John say of such, "Ye need not that any man should teach you; but the annointing which ye have received, teacheth you of all things. The teaching of the Holy Ghost brings out passages in the Bible, which had seemed meaningless and bare.

We can never know too much of that literature which throws side-lights on the Bible; and which unfolds the customs of the people, difficult allusions, historical coincidences, geographical details. Geikie's *Hours with the Bible;* Kitto's *Daily Illustrations,* edited by Dr. Porter; Dr. Smith's *Bible Dictionary:* books like these are invaluable. But we should study them at other times than in the morning hour, reserved for the Holy Ghost alone.

3. — *Read the Bible methodically.* For some reasons it is very helpful to map out the Bible into Annual Courses, and then neatly insert the dates, once for all, in the margin as a permanent guide. The Old Testament forms two Annual Courses, each portion averaging five -sixths of a page of a Bagster's Bible; while the New Testament makes a single course, each day's reading being on an average exactly one column.

This system has been adopted by those members of the Y.M.C.A. Bible Beading Union not already pledged to use other portions; and by other friends who use the tasteful little "Calendars" (one for each Testament) in which the Annual Courses are clearly arranged. The short New Testament portions should be read every year by all; and *one* Old Testament course by all who can possibly do so, thus working the larger division of the Sacred Volume through in two years.

It is wise to have a good copy of the Scriptures, strongly bound for wear and tear; of good clear print, and with as much space as possible for notes. It is wise at first to select one with copious marginal references; so that it may be easy to turn to the parallel passages. For myself, this plan has invested my Bible reading with new interest. I love to have in front of me one of the Paragraph Bibles of the Religious Tract Society, which abound in well-chosen references, and a small pocket Bible in my hand, that I may easily turn to any reference I desire; and very often I get more blessing from the passages to which I refer, and those to which these lead, than from the one I may be reading.

After a while, we shall begin to make references for ourselves; and then we may use a copy of the Revised Bible; that we may not only be able to read God's Word in the most approved English rendering, which is an immense advantage; but that we may also be able to fill up the empty margins with the notes of parallel passages.

But whatever system is adopted, be sure to read the Bible through on some system as you would read any other book. No one would think of reading a letter, poem, or history, as many read God's Word. What wonder that they are so ignorant of its majestic prose, its exquisite lyric poetry, its massive arguments, its sublime imagery, its spiritual beauty — qualities which combine to make it the King of Books, even though the halo of Inspiration did not shine like a crown about its brow!

It is sometimes well to read a book at a sitting, devoting two or three hours to the sacred task. At other times, it is more profitable to take an epoch, or an episode, or a life, and compare all that is written of it in various parts of Scripture. At other times, again, it is well to follow the plan, on which Mr. Moody has so often insisted, of taking one word or thought, as Faith, or Love, or Able, and tracing it, by help of a concordance, from end to end of the inspired volume. But in any case, let the *whole* Bible be your study; because "*All* Scripture is given by inspiration of God, and is profitable." Even the rocky places shall gush with water-springs. The most barren chapters shall blossom as the rose. "Out of the eater shall come forth meat, and sweetness out of the strong."

Let us never forget that the Bible is one Book; the work of one Infinite Spirit, speaking through Prophet and Priest, Shepherd and King, the old-world Patriarch and the Apostle who lived to see Jerusalem leveled to the ground. You may subject its words to the most searching test, but you will find they will always bear the same meaning, and move in the same direction. Let the Bible be its own Dictionary, its own Interpreter, its own best Commentary. It is like a vast buried city, in which every turn of the spade reveals some new marvel, whilst passages branch off in every direction calling for exploration.

4. — *Read your Bible with your pen in hand*. Writing of F. R. Havergal, her sister says, "She read her Bible at her study table by seven o'clock in the summer, and eight o'clock in winter; sometimes, on bitterly cold mornings, I begged that she would read with her feet comfortably to the fire, and received the reply: 'But then, Marie, I can't rule my lines neatly; just see what a find I've got!' If only one searches, there are such extraordinary things in the Bible. She resolutely refrained from late hours and frittering talks at night in place of Bible searching and holy communings. Early rising and early studying were her rule through life."

None, in my judgment, have learnt the secret of enjoying the Bible until they have commenced to mark it, neatly. Underlining and dating special verses, which have cast a light upon their path on special days. Drawing railway connections, across the page, between verses, which repeat the same message, or ring with the same note. Jotting down new references, or the catchwords of helpful thoughts. All these methods find plenty of employment for the pen; and fix our treasures for us permanently. Our Bible then becomes the precious memento of bye-gone hours; and records the history of our inner life.

5. — *Seek eagerly your Personal Profit.* Do not read the Bible for others, for class or congregation; but for yourself. Bring all its rays to a focus on your own heart. Whilst you are reading, often ask that some verse or verses may start out from the printed page, as God's message to yourself. And never close the book until you feel that you are carrying away your portion of meat from that Hand which satisfieth the desire of every living thing. It is well sometimes to stop reading, and seriously ask, What does the Holy Spirit mean *me* to learn by this; what bearing should this have on *my* life; how can I work this into the fabric of *my* character?

Let not the Bible be to you simply as a history, a treatise, or a poem, but as your Father's letter to yourself; in which there are some things which you will not understand, till you come into the circumstances which require them; but which is also full of present help. There is a great difference between the way in which an absent child scans the parcel of newspapers, and that in which he devours the Home-letter, by which the beloved parent speaks. Both are interesting, but the one is general, the other is all to himself. Read the Bible, not as a newspaper, but as a Home-letter.

Above all, turn from the printed page to prayer. If a cluster of heavenly fruit hangs within reach, gather it. If a promise lies upon the page as a blank cheque, cash it. If a prayer is recorded, appropriate it, and launch it as a feathered arrow from the bow of your desire. If an example of holiness gleams before you, ask God to do as much for you. If a truth is revealed in all its intrinsic splendor, entreat that its brilliance may even irradiate the hemisphere of your life like a star. Entwine the climbing creepers of holy desire about the lattice-work of Scripture. So shall you come to say with the Psalmist, "Oh, how I love Thy law, it is my meditation all the day!"

It is sometimes well to read over, on our knees. Psalm cxix. so full of devout love for the Bible. And if any should chide us for spending so much time upon the Old Testament, or the New, let us remind them of the words of Christ, "Man shall not live by bread alone, but by every word that proceedeth out of the mouth of God." The Old Testament must be worth our study since it was our Saviour's Bible deeply pondered and often quoted. And the New demands it, since it is so full of what He said and did, not only in His earthly life, but through the medium of His holy apostles and prophets.

The advantages of a deep knowledge of the Bible are more than can be numbered here. It is the Storehouse of the Promises It is the Sword of the Spirit before which temptation flees. It is the all-sufficient Equipment for Christian usefulness. It is the believer's Guide-book and Directory m all possible circumstances. Words fail to tell how glad, how strong, how useful shall be the daily life of those who can say with the Prophet, "Thy words were found, and I did eat them; and Thy word was unto me the joy and rejoicing of my

But there is one thing, which may be said last, because it is most important, and should linger in the memory and heart, though all the other exhortations of this tractlet should pass away as a summer-brook. It is this. It is useless to dream of making headway in the knowledge of Scripture, unless we are prepared to practice each new and clearly-defined duty, which looms out before our view. We are taught, not for our pleasure only, *but that we may do*. If we will turn each holy precept or command into instant obedience, through the dear grace of Jesus Christ our Lord, God will keep nothing back from us; He will open to us His deepest and sweetest thoughts. But so long as we refuse obedience to even the least command, we shall find that the light will fade from the page of Scripture, and the zest will die down quickly in our own hearts.

"This Book of the Law shall not depart out of thy mouth, but thou shalt meditate therein day and night, that thou mayest observe to do according to all that is written therein: for then thou shalt make thy way prosperous, and then thou shalt have good success" (Joshua i. 8).

A Keswick Experience

ONE memorable evening, towards the close of a convention of unusual power, a quiet, eager crowd of some twelve hundred people gathered in the great tent to seek a fresh enduement of the Holy Spirit. The time was spent in prayer and praise, and quotation of Scripture expressive of experiences which were lifting many to the open gate of Paradise. As I knelt in a retired corner of the platform, I realized that the Lord was coming manifestly and sensibly to many of His temples, for the fact of His presence was attested by their almost tumultuous joy. But in all this I had no share other than to long with vehement desire to be included in the gifts which were being so bountifully bestowed. I was suffering at the time from nervous depression, the reaction from a long spell of work; and it seemed to me as though I were standing in some outer circle, with which I must be content, whilst those whose emotional life was more exuberant, were participating in spiritual communications of the rarest type. At last I could bear it no longer, and whilst the meeting was still proceeding I slipped through the tent curtains into the night, speaking to no one, and only eager to be away on those hills which to so many have been Pisgahs of vision and Hermons of transfiguration.

During the week, beneath the searching light of those eyes which are as a flame of fire, I had put away what had been revealed of the filthiness of the flesh and spirit, and there was therefore no reason why the blessing should be delayed. When I reached a familiar spot, I cried aloud: — "My Father, if there is one soul more than another within the circle of these hills that needs the gift of Pentecost, it is I; but I am too weary to think, or feel, or pray intensely. Is it not possible to receive it without the tide of emotion which so often accompanies its advent or renewal in the soul?"

Then a voice, sweet and low, seemed to say, "Claim and receive it by an act of faith, apart from feeling. As thy share in God's forgiving grace was won for thee by the dying Christ, so thy share in the pentecostal gift is held for thee by the glorified Christ; and as thou didst take the former, so thou must take the latter, and reckon that it is thine, by a faith which is utterly indifferent to the presence or absence of resulting joy. According to thy faith, so it will be done unto thee." Then it seemed to me as if I took a deep inspiration of that wind which bloweth where it listeth. I opened my mouth and panted. I took from the hands of the living Christ my share, or as much of it as I could then receive, of the fullness of the Spirit, which the Father had entrusted to Him on my behalf; and as I turned to retrace my steps to the town I dared to reckon that it was mine as never before.

On my way to take a farewell glimpse of the lake, it being about midnight, I came on a group of friends, engaged in discussing the meetings of the day and the all-engrossing theme of how to receive the Pentecostal gift. They were full of holy ecstasy, in strong contrast to my own recent experience, and seemed astonished at the thought that the same breath of God had not elicited a similar rapturous response as it swept the chords of my heart.

And so we passed through the swing-gate, and by the side of the church, rearing itself above us in somber silence, and came on the terrace, from which we could see Derwentwater gleaming below, at the foot of the encircling hills. The night-clouds were sweeping over it, veiling the stars and descending at intervals in light showers of rain. So we drew two forms together, and gathering close began to compare our experience.

All alike confessed their liability to alternations of feeling, and even relapse in the inner life, when the conditions of soul-health were neglected; but they laid a considerable stress on emotion as the test of their spiritual condition, and especially on the consciousness of joy or power in attesting the reception of the Holy Spirit. They reckoned that they were filled of the Spirit, so far as they felt His strivings and workings within; whereas, as I had received Him without emotion, I might expect ever to retain and enlarge its measure, whether the song-birds of summer or the stillness of winter occupied my heart.

After we had gone round the little circle, and every one had recited the sacred inner story, a young business-man broke in somehow thus: "Is there not a danger of your fixing your attention too much on the Holy Spirit and His methods and too little on Him whom the Spirit came to reveal and glorify? My experience of the Holy Spirit is that He reveals Christ. It is the one desire of my life that He should make the Lord real to me; then sin cannot tempt or danger frighten. I am a business-man; and if I lose the sense of His presence for half an hour, I lock myself into my counting-house and ask the Holy Spirit what I have done to grieve Him and cause Him to veil that radiance from my heart." "That's it," we all exclaimed; "it is more of Jesus that we need. The Spirit is come to bear witness of and glorify Him." Then we bent our heads, and under a strong impulse humbly claimed that we might so receive the Holy Spirit that, whatever our company, or engagements, or experiences, Jesus might increasingly become the dear Companion and Guide of our lives.

* * * *

Are *you* living in the power of the Pentecostal gift of the Holy Spirit? His advent on the Day of Pentecost was a distinct historical event, as distinct and as definite as the advent of our Lord to Bethlehem. You are living in the enjoyment of the blessings resulting from the latter; are you living also in the full experience of those which have accrued from the former? If not, you are missing the distinctive mark of Christianity, which gives it a unique position among all the religions of the world.

The Apostles believed in Christ and called Him Master and Lord before Pentecost. In doing so, they bore witness to the operation of the Holy Spirit in their hearts. He had been working in the hearts of men from the beginning. But there was an immense difference between what they were up to the Day of Pentecost and what they became as soon as the Spirit had come. It is evidently possible, then, for a man to be a believer in Christ, and even to own Him Lord, through the gracious work of the Holy Ghost; and yet he may miss the deeper experiences of which Pentecost was the sign and seal. Is this your case?

On which side of Pentecost are you living? Historically, no doubt, you live on the hither side of that great day; but experimentally and practically you may be living on the other. You are in the great light, but you don't see it; you are in a gold region, but you are none the richer for it. Before you stands an open door into the heart of Divine knowledge and power, but you have never essayed to enter it. Whilst thousands are living practically as though Jesus had never been incarnate, died, and risen, you are living much as you would have done had the gift of Pentecost never been bestowed. Think! Is there anything in your Christian life that would have been different if the hour of Pentecost had never struck?

If not, be sure that there is something in Christianity that you have never tasted. There is a dividend awaiting you under Christ's new testament which you have never claimed, but which, if once apprehended and appropriated, would make your life rich, fragrant, and vocal as a garden in May.

There are several tests by which you may know whether you have participated in that filling of the Holy Spirit which is characteristic of the Pentecostal gift. Among these are the following:—

1. — *A consciousness of the presence of Christ.* Mr. Spurgeon said once that he never passed a single quarter of an hour in his waking moments without a distinct consciousness of the presence of the Lord. When the Spirit fills the

heart, Jesus is vividly real and evidently near. What is He to you? Do you wake in the morning beneath His light touch and spend the hours with Him? Can you frequently look up from your work and perceive His face? Are you constantly seeking from Him power, grace, direction? If He is but a fitful vision, you have not realized the first mark of the Pentecostal gift.

2. — *Deliverance from the power of sin.* The Holy Ghost is like fire. As fire cleanses metal, so does He the heart. When He is within the heart in power, the air is so rarefied that the germs of contagion are rendered harmless. When the spirit is filled with the Holy Spirit, it will be conscious of temptation, more keenly alive to its least approach than ever before; but it will have no fascination, no power. People talk much of a clean heart; it seems to me wiser and truer to speak of the Holy Spirit as Indweller and Cleanser, whose presence is purity.

3. — *Minute and direct guidance.* Not mere vagary or impulse, but guidance, in harmony with the word of God on one hand and the drift or trend of circumstances on the other. But we must be more quiet before God to detect it. Dr. Pierson showed me in his study at Philadelphia an armchair with special associations. He had been comforting a brother-minister, who had been confined to his bed for six months, by suggesting that perhaps God had been compelled to lay him aside in order to get an opportunity of saying things which in his busy life he was unable to receive. Then suddenly the thought occurred to him that he too was giving God but few opportunities of communicating His will, and he resolved that thenceforth he would spend at least half an hour each night sitting before God when his family had retired and the house was still. He said that during those times of retirement he had been distinctly-conscious that God spoke with him and told him His will. If you are not led by the Spirit, be sure that you are not filled by Him.

4. — *Power in service.* There is a difference between the Spirit being *in* and *on* us. It is the same Spirit, though in two different manifestations of His grace. Some have the Spirit of God in them for character, but they are not gifted by Him for service. Our Lord Jesus, though conceived of the Holy Ghost, yet stood beneath the opened heavens to be anointed of the Spirit before He entered on His public ministry; and the Church was held back from her work of evangelizing the waiting world until she had received the Pentecostal enduement of power. Yet how many Christians are attempting to do this work without this power.

When speaking on this theme to a recent students' convention at Northfield, Mr. Moody was completely broken down, and in utterances choked with weeping confessed that he was deeply conscious of his lack of this special power. The whole of the students broke down too, and he asked them to give up the customary afternoon sports and to meet him. in the neighboring woods, that they might together seek a fresh anointing for service. Are we conscious of possessing this qualification for soul-winning? If not, why do you not claim your share of the Pentecostal life from your Trustee and Representative?

* * * *

We often wish that we could have been amongst the favored group when the Day of Pentecost had fully come and they were all together in the upper room. We think that we should, of course, have heard the sound as of the rushing of a mighty wind and received on our brows the encircling flame, in our hearts the blessed filling. But in all likelihood, if we had been there in our present condition, the hurricane of blessing would have swept past, leaving us dry and insensible. Whilst if that Pentecostal group were living now, they would detect as much of the Spirit's presence, they would be as conscious of the working of the Lord Jesus, they would find life as full of God, as in the days when the age was young. Peter would still be filled with the Holy Ghost and speak; Paul would be caught up into the seventh heaven and need a thorn to counterbalance the splendor of the revelations; John would find doors opening into heaven, amid the conditions of our modern life, not less than when the chime of the Aegean rose from the beach of Patmos.

A change, you say, is needed. But there need be no change in your circumstances, in the atmosphere or environment of your life. There is as much of the Holy Ghost within your reach as was present on the Day of Pentecost. This is the age of Pentecost. He waits to fill you as He did the hundred and twenty gathered in the upper room. The miraculous gifts have passed away because no longer needed. They are replaced by evidences that were not possible in those early days. But the essence of the Pentecostal gift, the filling of the Spirit, is as possible to-day as ever. "The promise," said the Apostle, alluding to our Saviour's words, "is unto all that are afar off, even as many as the Lord our God shall call" (Acts i. 4; ii. 39).

But of what use is it to live in a very ocean of power and love if we are unable to discern its presence or appropriate its marvelous properties? Of what use is it that the land of the Hottentots is as full of electricity as London is if they know not and cannot use its mighty energy? Of what use is it that the summer days are full of dews, and heat, and light, and other materials out of which peaches and nectarines are made if there are no peach-blossoms nestling on the boughs to detect or use them? Of what use is it that the floor is covered with nourishing food if the newborn babe which lies beside it is unconscious of its existence and incapable of assimilating it?

There is no need, then, to sigh for the lost age of gold, since the King of all ages is here. Had we lived with Him in His earthly life, the benefit would have been infinitesimal apart from *appropriating faith;* but if we have *that,* though we see Him not, we may secure His choicest gifts. These conditions, however, must be fulfilled before you can exercise that faith and receive that supreme gift: —

1. — *Be careful that you desire the filling of the Holy Spirit only for the glory of God.* If you want it that you may realize a certain experience, or attract

people to yourself, or transform some difficulty into a steppingstone, you are likely to miss it. You must be set on the one purpose of magnifying the Lord Jesus in your body, whether by life or death. Ask that all inferior motives may be destroyed, and that this may burn strong and clear within you.

2. — *Be cleansed from all sin of which you may be conscious.* If you have grieved God by impurity, or anger, or unkind judgments of others, seek forgiveness, restoration, and cleansing. The cleansed heart is an essential of Spirit-filling.

3. — *Present yourself and your members to God.* There should be no reserve, no locked cupboards, no closed doors, no vault barricaded from sun and air by a great slab of stone. Open every door and window of your being to the Holy Spirit, and He will certainly come in, though you may not be aware of the moment or method of His entrance.

4. — *Give time to prayer and meditation on the word of God.* There is no such way of communing with God as to walk to and fro in your own room or in the open air, your Bible in hand, meditating on it and turning its precepts and promises into prayer. God walks in the glades of Scripture, as of old in those of Paradise.

5. — *Then by faith reverently and humbly take the Father's gift through Jesus Christ.* Let it be a definite transaction. Ask for the filling of the Spirit, after the measure of Pentecost. Dip your bucket deep down into the brimming well and bring it back dripping with crystal drops. Reckon that God has answered your prayer and has granted the petition you made. Meet every suggestion of doubt by the decisive answer that God is faithful and must do as He has said. But specially dare to act faith, going to the temptation in the desert or the ministry among men assured that you have received all the equipment that you could possibly require.

Whenever you are conscious of leakage; when the exhaustion of service has been greater than the reception of fresh supplies; when some new avenue of ministry, or freshly discovered talent, or new department of your being, has presented itself, go again to the same source for a refilling, a recharging with spiritual power, a re-anointing by the holy chrism.

Three tenses are used in the Acts of the Apostles of the filling of the Spirit, which have their counterparts still: —

Filled: a sudden decisive experience for a specific work (Acts iv. 8).

Were being filled: the imperfect tense, as though the blessed process were always going on (Acts xiii. 52).

Full: the adjective, indicating the perpetual experience (Acts vi. 8).

www.ingramcontent.com/pod-product-compliance
Lightning Source LLC
LaVergne TN
LVHW091313080426
835510LV00007B/481